All Time

FAMILY FAVORITES™

COUNTRY CHRISTMAS

PUBLICATIONS INTERNATIONAL, LTD.

Louis Weber, C.E.O.
Publications International, Ltd.
7373 N. Cicero Ave.
Lincolnwood, IL 60646

Some of the products listed in this publication may be in limited distribution.

Front cover photography by Sacco Productions Limited, Chicago.

Pictured on the front cover *(clockwise from top left):* Cranberry Raisin Nut Bread *(page 26)*, Cranberry-Orange Relish *(page 54)*, Christmas Citrus Marmalade *(page 48)*, Freezer Plum Conserve *(page 54)*, Carrot & Coriander Soup *(page 14)*, Raspberry Vinegar *(page 52)*, Herbed Vinegar *(page 52)*, Country Pecan Pie *(page 100)*, Holiday Sugar Cookies *(page 62)*, Gingerbread People *(page 68)*, Almond Crescents *(page 70)* and Pecan Cheese Ball *(page 8)*.

Pictured on the back cover *(top box):* Dark Chocolate Fudge *(page 92)* and Peanut Butter Fudge *(page 92); (middle box):* Traditional Peanut Brittle *(page 92)*.

ISBN: 0-7853-1310-9

Manufactured in U.S.A.

8 7 6 5 4 3 2 1

Microwave Cooking: Microwave ovens may vary in wattage. The microwave cooking times given in this publication are approximate. Use the cooking times as guidelines and check for doneness before adding more time. Consult manufacturer's instructions for suitable microwave-safe dishes.

Contents

— Sensational —

SEASONAL STARTERS

SMUCKER'S® CELEBRATION BRIE

1 round (12 to 16 ounces) brie cheese, at room temperature
1 teaspoon coarsely ground black pepper
½ cup SMUCKER'S® Strawberry Preserves
1 tablespoon balsamic vinegar
½ cup chopped figs
Assorted crackers

Sprinkle top of brie with pepper; press gently into cheese. Mix preserves with vinegar; stir in figs. Spoon mixture over cheese. Serve with assorted crackers.

Makes 12 servings

CHEESE TWISTS

- 1 cup all-purpose flour
- ½ teaspoon baking soda
- ½ teaspoon dry mustard
- ½ teaspoon salt
- ⅛ teaspoon ground red pepper
- ¾ cup grated Parmesan cheese, divided
- ½ cup butter or margarine, softened
- 3 egg yolks
- 2 teaspoons water
- 1 egg white, slightly beaten
- 1 tablespoon sesame seeds (optional)

Preheat oven to 400°F. Grease two cookie sheets. Combine flour, baking soda, mustard, salt and red pepper in large bowl. Reserve 1 tablespoon cheese; stir remaining cheese into flour mixture. Cut in butter with pastry blender or 2 knives until mixture resembles fine crumbs. Add egg yolks and water, mixing until dough forms. Shape into a ball; flatten and wrap in plastic wrap. Refrigerate 2 hours or until firm.

Roll out dough on lightly floured surface into 12-inch square (about ⅛ inch thick). Brush surface lightly with egg white and sprinkle with remaining 1 tablespoon cheese and sesame seeds, if desired. Cut dough in half. Cut each half crosswise into ¼-inch strips. Twist 2 strips together. Repeat with remaining strips. Place 1 inch apart on prepared cookie sheets. Bake 6 to 8 minutes until light golden brown. Remove from cookie sheets and cool completely on wire racks. Store in airtight container.

Makes about 48 twists

VARIATION: Prepare dough and cut as directed. Place ¾ of strips on cookie sheets. Form rings with remaining strips; seal edges. Place on cookie sheets. Bake and cool as directed. To serve, arrange 3 to 4 strips into small stacks. Insert stacks into rings.

DEVILED MIXED NUTS

- 3 tablespoons vegetable oil
- 2 cups assorted unsalted nuts, such as peanuts, almonds, Brazil nuts or walnuts
- 2 tablespoons sugar
- 1 teaspoon paprika
- ½ teaspoon ground chili powder
- ½ teaspoon curry powder
- ½ teaspoon ground cumin
- ½ teaspoon ground coriander
- ½ teaspoon ground black pepper
- ¼ teaspoon salt

Heat oil in large skillet over medium heat; cook and stir nuts in hot oil 2 to 3 minutes until browned. Combine remaining ingredients in small bowl; sprinkle over nuts. Stir to coat evenly. Heat 1 to 2 minutes more. Drain nuts on wire rack lined with paper towels. Serve warm.

Makes 6 to 8 servings or 2 cups nuts

Top to bottom: *Cheese Twists, Deviled Mixed Nuts and Marinated Mushrooms (page 10)*

PECAN CHEESE BALL

1 package (8 ounces) cream cheese, softened
¼ cup finely chopped parsley
2 tablespoons finely chopped chives
½ teaspoon Worcestershire sauce
Dash hot pepper sauce
¾ cup finely chopped pecans
Assorted crackers

Combine all ingredients except pecans and crackers in medium bowl. Cover; refrigerate until firm. Form cheese mixture into a ball. Roll in pecans. Store tightly wrapped in plastic wrap in refrigerator. Allow cheese ball to soften at room temperature before serving with crackers.

Makes 1 cheese ball

VARIATIONS: Form cheese mixture into 1½-inch balls. Roll in paprika, chopped herbs, such as parsley, watercress or basil, or chopped green olives instead of pecans.

GIFT TIP: Give Pecan Cheese Ball with an assortment of other cheeses, a wooden cheese board, a jar of imported pickles or mustard and/or a bag of pecans.

FESTIVE STUFFED DATES

1 box (8 ounces) DOLE® Whole Pitted Dates
1 package (3 ounces) light cream cheese
¼ cup powdered sugar
Grated peel from 1 DOLE® Orange

• Make slit in center of each date.

• Combine cream cheese, powdered sugar and 1 tablespoon orange peel. Fill center of dates with cream cheese mixture. Refrigerate.

• Dust with additional powdered sugar just before serving, if desired. *Makes about 27 stuffed dates*

Prep Time: 25 minutes

SAUSAGE CHEESE PUFFS

1 pound BOB EVANS FARMS® Original Recipe Roll Sausage
2½ cups (10 ounces) shredded sharp Cheddar cheese
2 cups biscuit mix
½ cup water
1 teaspoon baking powder

Preheat oven to 350°F. Combine ingredients in large bowl until blended. Shape into 1-inch balls. Place on lightly greased baking sheets. Bake about 25 minutes or until golden brown. Serve hot. Refrigerate leftovers. *Makes about 60 appetizers*

SWEET 'N' SOUR MEATBALLS

1 pound lean ground beef
1 cup soft bread crumbs
1 egg, slightly beaten
2 tablespoons minced onion
2 tablespoons milk
1 clove garlic, minced
½ teaspoon salt
⅛ teaspoon black pepper
1 tablespoon vegetable oil
⅔ cup HEINZ® Chili Sauce
⅔ cup red currant or grape jelly

Combine first 8 ingredients; form into 40 bite-sized meatballs, using a full teaspoon for each. Brown meatballs in oil. Cover; cook over low heat 5 minutes. Drain excess fat. Combine chili sauce and jelly; pour over meatballs. Heat, stirring occasionally, until jelly is melted. Simmer 10 to 12 minutes until sauce has thickened, basting occasionally. *Makes 40 appetizers (¾ cup sauce)*

CLAM DIP

1 package (3 ounces) cream cheese, softened
1 cup dairy sour cream
1 can (6½ ounces) minced clams
2 teaspoons lemon juice
1½ teaspoons Worcestershire sauce
½ teaspoon LAWRY'S® Seasoned Salt
Dash LAWRY'S® Seasoned Pepper

In medium bowl, blend cream cheese and sour cream. Drain clams and reserve 1 tablespoon clam juice. Add clams and reserved clam juice to sour cream mixture. Add remaining ingredients and blend well. *Makes 1½ cups*

PRESENTATION: Serve with crisp, raw vegetables and Johannisberg Riesling.

HINT: For a thinner dip, add more clam juice.

WISCONSIN CHEDDAR SCONES WITH SMOKED TURKEY

4 cups biscuit mix
2½ cups (10 ounces) finely shredded Wisconsin sharp Cheddar cheese
1¼ cups milk
2 eggs
¼ cup butter, melted
Smoked turkey, thinly sliced

Preheat oven to 400°F.

Combine biscuit mix, cheese, milk, eggs and butter; mix well until ingredients are moistened. Drop by tablespoonfuls onto lightly greased baking sheet. Bake 12 to 14 minutes or until golden brown. Remove from oven; cool slightly before removing from baking sheet. To serve, slice scones in half and fill with sliced turkey. Arrange on serving tray. *Makes 32 appetizers*

Favorite recipe from ***Wisconsin Milk Marketing Board***

CORN AND TOMATO CHOWDER

1½ cups peeled and diced plum tomatoes
¾ teaspoon salt, divided
2 ears corn, husks removed
1 tablespoon margarine
½ cup finely chopped shallots
1 clove garlic, minced
1 cup chicken broth
1 can (12 ounces) evaporated skimmed milk
¼ teaspoon black pepper
1 tablespoon finely chopped fresh sage *or* 1 teaspoon rubbed sage
1 tablespoon cornstarch
2 tablespoons cold water

Place tomatoes in nonmetal colander over bowl. Sprinkle ½ teaspoon salt on top; toss to mix well. Allow tomatoes to drain at least 1 hour.

Meanwhile, cut corn kernels off the cobs into small bowl. Scrape cobs, with dull side of knife, to "milk" liquid from cobs into same bowl; set aside. Discard 1 cob; break remaining cob in half.

Heat margarine in heavy medium saucepan over medium-high heat until melted and bubbly. Add shallots and garlic; reduce heat to low. Cover and cook about 5 minutes or until shallots are soft and translucent. Add broth, milk, black pepper, sage and reserved corn cob halves. Bring to a boil over high heat. Reduce heat to low; simmer, uncovered, 10 minutes. Remove and discard cob halves. Add corn; return to a boil over medium-high heat. Reduce heat to low; simmer, uncovered, 15 minutes more. Dissolve cornstarch in water; add to chowder, mixing well. Stir until thickened. Remove from heat; stir in drained tomatoes and remaining ¼ teaspoon salt. Spoon into bowls. Garnish with additional fresh sage, if desired.

Makes 6 appetizer servings

MARINATED MUSHROOMS

1 pint uniformly sized small white button mushroom caps, washed and left whole
½ cup olive oil
3 tablespoons tarragon vinegar
¼ cup finely chopped parsley
1 tablespoon Dijon mustard
3 cloves garlic, finely chopped
1 teaspoon sugar
¾ teaspoon dried tarragon leaves
½ teaspoon salt
Freshly ground black pepper

Fill 16-ounce jar with mushrooms, arranging attractively. Process remaining ingredients in food processor or combine in small bowl with wire whisk. Pour dressing into jar to cover mushrooms completely. Seal jar and marinate overnight to blend flavors. Store up to 1 week in refrigerator.

Makes about 6 servings or 3 cups

Corn and Tomato Chowder

SHRIMP DIP

1 package (8 ounces) cream cheese, softened
½ cup HEINZ® Seafood Cocktail Sauce
2 tablespoons plain yogurt
2 tablespoons minced green onion
1½ teaspoons HEINZ® Worcestershire Sauce
¼ teaspoon garlic powder
1 can (4½ ounces) small shrimp, rinsed, drained*
Potato chips, crackers or raw vegetables

*¾ cup chopped cooked shrimp may be substituted.

Combine first 6 ingredients; stir in shrimp. Chill several hours or overnight. Serve with chips, crackers or vegetables. *Makes about 2 cups*

HOLIDAY PÂTÉ

1 package (8 ounces) JONES® Braunschweiger
1 package (3 ounces) cream cheese
1 tablespoon finely chopped onion
1 tablespoon Worcestershire sauce
1 to 2 tablespoons dry sherry
⅓ to ½ teaspoon ground nutmeg
Dash of hot pepper sauce (to taste)

Blend all ingredients and serve with crackers or bread. *Makes about 1¼ cups*

SWEET PEPPER GARLIC SOUP

2 teaspoons olive oil
½ cup chopped onion
6 cloves garlic, chopped
1 cup cubed unpeeled potato
1 cup chopped red bell peppers
3½ cups ⅓-less-salt chicken broth
1 cup low fat cottage cheese
2 tablespoons plain nonfat yogurt
⅛ teaspoon black pepper

Heat oil in medium saucepan over medium heat; add onion and garlic. Cook and stir 3 minutes or until onion is tender. Add potato, bell peppers and broth. Bring to a boil; reduce heat and simmer 10 to 15 minutes or until potato is easily pierced when tested with fork. Remove from heat; cool completely.

Place broth mixture in food processor or blender; process until smooth. Refrigerate until completely cool.

Place cottage cheese and yogurt in food processor or blender; process until smooth. Set aside ¼ cup cheese mixture. Stir remaining cheese mixture into chilled broth mixture until well blended. Add black pepper; stir well. Top with reserved cheese mixture. Garnish with parsley and bell pepper strips, if desired. *Makes 6 (¾-cup) servings*

Sweet Pepper Garlic Soup

CHEDDAR CHEESE SPREAD

3 ounces each white Cheddar, yellow Cheddar and cream cheese, cut into small pieces
6 green onions, white parts only, finely chopped
2 tablespoons butter or margarine, softened
2 tablespoons dry sherry
1 teaspoon Worcestershire sauce
1 teaspoon Dijon mustard
¼ teaspoon salt (optional)
Dash hot pepper sauce (optional)
2 tablespoons finely chopped chives
Assorted crackers

Place all ingredients except chives and crackers in food processor or blender; process until smooth. Add chives; pulse to mix in. Place in crock or gift container. Cover; refrigerate. Allow spread to soften at room temperature before serving. Serve with crackers. *Makes about 2 cups spread*

GIFT TIP: Include a box of crackers with the crock of spread.

CARROT & CORIANDER SOUP

4 tablespoons butter or margarine
4 cups grated carrots (about 1 pound)
1 cup finely chopped onion
3 cups chicken broth
2 tablespoons fresh lemon juice
1½ teaspoons ground coriander
1½ teaspoons ground cumin
1 clove garlic, finely chopped
2 tablespoons finely chopped fresh coriander (cilantro)
Salt and black pepper

Heat butter in medium saucepan over medium-high heat until melted and bubbly. Cook and stir carrots and onion in hot butter 5 minutes or until onion begins to soften. Add broth, lemon juice, ground coriander, cumin and garlic. Bring to a boil over high heat. Reduce heat to low. Cover; simmer 25 to 30 minutes until vegetables are soft.

Process soup in batches in food processor or blender until smooth. Stir in fresh coriander. Season to taste with salt and pepper. Serve immediately or cool and pour into clean glass jars; seal tightly. Store up to 1 week in refrigerator. Reheat before serving. *Makes 4 to 6 servings*

Cinnamon Parsnip Soup

- 2 tablespoons margarine or unsalted butter
- 1 medium onion, chopped
- 2 pounds parsnips, peeled and cut into 2-inch chunks
- 3 cups chicken broth
- ½ cup dry white wine
- ½ cup half-and-half
- ¼ teaspoon TABASCO® pepper sauce
- Ground cinnamon

• In 3- to 4-quart saucepan, combine margarine and onion. Cook over medium-high heat, stirring often, about 5 minutes or until onion is translucent.

• Add parsnips and broth. Bring to a boil over high heat. Reduce heat; cover and simmer about 30 minutes or until parsnips are very tender.

• Process mixture, a portion at a time, in food processor or blender until smooth. Return to saucepan. Stir in wine, half-and-half and TABASCO sauce; heat until steaming.

• Sprinkle individual servings with cinnamon.

Makes 4 to 6 servings

Bacon Horseradish Dip

- 1 container (16 ounces) BREAKSTONE'S® Sour Cream
- 1 can (3 ounces) OSCAR MAYER® Real Bacon Bits
- 1 tablespoon Worcestershire sauce
- 1 tablespoon prepared horseradish
- ½ teaspoon hot pepper sauce
- Dash garlic powder

• Mix all ingredients in medium bowl. Cover; refrigerate at least 1 hour to blend flavors.

• Serve with crackers, chips or assorted raw vegetables.

Makes 2¼ cups

Creamy Brick Spread

- 8 ounces Wisconsin Brick cheese, shredded
- 8 ounces cream cheese with chives and onion, softened
- ½ teaspoon hot pepper sauce
- Cocktail rye, pumpernickel bread, crisp crackers or bagel crisps

Combine brick cheese, cream cheese and hot pepper sauce; blend until smooth. Warm in microwave oven, if desired. Serve with cocktail rye.

Makes 1½ cups spread

Favorite recipe from ***Wisconsin Milk Marketing Board***

RED BEAN SOUP

1 pound dried red kidney beans
1 sprig fresh thyme
1 sprig fresh parsley
2 tablespoons butter or margarine
1 small onion, finely chopped
4 carrots, peeled and chopped
2 ribs celery, chopped
1½ quarts water
1 pound smoked ham hocks
1 bay leaf
3 cloves garlic, finely chopped
½ teaspoon salt
¼ teaspoon black pepper
2 tablespoons fresh lemon juice
Dairy sour cream, for garnish
"Holly leaf" and "berry" cutouts, made from green and red bell peppers (optional)

Soak beans in 1 quart water in large bowl 6 hours or overnight. Drain; rinse and set aside. Tie together thyme and parsley sprigs with thread; set aside.

Heat butter in heavy, large stockpot over medium-high heat until melted and bubbly. Cook and stir onion in hot butter 3 minutes or until onion is softened. Add carrots and celery; cook and stir 5 minutes or until browned. Add 1½ quarts water, beans, ham, bay leaf, garlic and reserved thyme and parsley sprigs. Bring to a boil over high heat. Reduce heat to low. Cover; simmer 1¼ to 1½ hours until beans are softened. Discard bones, thyme and parsley sprigs and bay leaf. Stir in salt and pepper.

Process soup in batches in food processor or blender until smooth. Return to stockpot. Heat to simmering; stir in lemon juice and season to taste with additional salt and pepper. Ladle into bowls. Garnish with sour cream and green pepper "leaves" and red pepper "berries," if desired.

Makes 6 servings

GIFT TIP: Give this soup in an attractive glass jar accompanied by soup bowls. Store up to 1 week in refrigerator. Reheat before serving.

BLACK BEAN SOUP: Substitute black beans for the red kidney beans. Proceed as directed, simmering soup 1½ to 2 hours or until beans are tender. Add 4 to 5 tablespoons sherry, to taste, just before serving.

CRANBERRY BEAN SOUP: Substitute cranberry beans for the red kidney beans. Proceed as directed, simmering soup 2 to 2¼ hours or until beans are tender. (Cranberry beans can be found in specialty food stores. They are the color of cranberries but taste similar to kidney beans. Give soup with an extra box of cranberry beans for a gift idea. These beans are great in salads.)

Top to bottom: *Carrot & Coriander Soup (page 14) and Red Bean Soup*

Carrot & Coriander
Soup

CREAMY CUCUMBER–YOGURT DIP

- **1 cucumber**
- **Salt**
- **¼ cup chopped chives, divided**
- **1 package (8 ounces) cream cheese, softened**
- **¼ cup plain yogurt**
- **1 tablespoon fresh lemon juice**
- **1½ teaspoons dried mint leaves**
- **Freshly ground black pepper**
- **Assorted cut-up vegetables**

Peel cucumber; cut in half lengthwise. Scoop out seeds with teaspoon; discard. Finely chop cucumber. Lightly salt cucumber in small bowl; toss. Refrigerate 1 hour. Drain cucumber; dry on paper towels. Set aside.

Reserve 1 tablespoon chives for garnish. Place remaining 3 tablespoons chives, cream cheese, yogurt, lemon juice, mint and pepper in food processor or blender; process until smooth. Stir into cucumber. Cover; refrigerate 1 hour. Spoon dip into glass bowl or gift container; sprinkle reserved chives over top. Cover and store up to 2 days in refrigerator. Stir before serving with vegetables. *Makes about 2 cups dip*

SPICY COCKTAIL SAUCE

- **1 cup tomato ketchup**
- **2 cloves garlic, finely chopped**
- **1 tablespoon fresh lemon juice**
- **1 teaspoon prepared horseradish**
- **¾ teaspoon chili powder**
- **½ teaspoon salt**
- **¼ teaspoon hot pepper sauce *or* ⅛ teaspoon ground red pepper**

Combine all ingredients in medium bowl; blend well. Spoon into glass bowl and serve with cooked seafood or pour into clean glass jar and seal tightly. Store up to 1 year in refrigerator.

Makes 1⅓ cups sauce, enough for 1 pound of seafood

GIFT TIP: If you are giving this to someone who lives nearby, it would be a charming thought to present it with some chilled cooked fresh shrimp.

Top to bottom: *Creamy Cucumber-Yogurt Dip and Spicy Cocktail Sauce*

Holiday

SAUSAGE PINWHEELS

2 cups biscuit mix
½ cup milk
¼ cup butter or margarine, melted
1 pound BOB EVANS FARMS® Original Recipe Roll Sausage

Combine biscuit mix, milk and butter in large bowl until blended. Refrigerate 30 minutes. Divide dough into two portions. Roll out one portion on floured surface to ⅛-inch-thick rectangle, about 10×7 inches. Spread with half the sausage. Roll lengthwise into long roll. Repeat with remaining dough and sausage. Place rolls in freezer until hard enough to cut easily. Preheat oven to 400°F. Cut rolls into thin slices. Place on baking sheets. Bake 15 minutes or until golden brown. Serve hot. Refrigerate leftovers. *Makes about 48 appetizers*

SERVING SUGGESTIONS: This recipe may be doubled. Refreeze after slicing. When ready to serve, thaw slices in refrigerator and bake.

CHEESY POTATO SOUP

4 baking potatoes (about 1½ pounds)
2 tablespoons butter
1 medium onion, sliced
2 tablespoons all-purpose flour
1 teaspoon beef bouillon granules
2 cups water
1 can (12 ounces) evaporated milk
1 cup (4 ounces) shredded Wisconsin Brick cheese
1 teaspoon chopped fresh parsley
¾ teaspoon Worcestershire sauce
¾ teaspoon salt
¾ teaspoon black pepper

Microwave potatoes at HIGH until tender; cool. Place butter and onion in large microwavable bowl. Microwave at HIGH until tender, about 2 minutes. Stir in flour. Add bouillon granules and water; stir well. Microwave at HIGH 2 minutes until mixture is heated through. Scoop out potatoes leaving pieces in chunks. Add potatoes, evaporated milk, cheese, parsley, Worcestershire sauce, salt and pepper to hot mixture. Microwave at HIGH 2½ to 4 minutes until cheese is melted and soup is hot. *Makes 6 servings*

Favorite recipe from ***Wisconsin Milk Marketing Board***

Sausage Pinwheels

Cherry Eggnog Quick Bread

2½ cups all-purpose flour
¾ cup sugar
1 tablespoon baking powder
½ teaspoon ground nutmeg
1¼ cups prepared dairy eggnog
6 tablespoons butter or margarine, melted
2 eggs, slightly beaten
1 teaspoon vanilla
½ cup chopped pecans
½ cup chopped candied red cherries

Preheat oven to 350°F. Grease 9×5-inch loaf pan.

Combine flour, sugar, baking powder and nutmeg in large bowl. Stir eggnog, butter, eggs and vanilla in medium bowl until well blended. Add eggnog mixture to flour mixture. Mix just until all ingredients are moistened. Stir in pecans and cherries. Spoon into prepared pan.

Bake 45 to 50 minutes until wooden pick inserted in center comes out clean. Cool in pan 15 minutes. Remove from pan and cool completely on wire rack. Store tightly wrapped in plastic wrap at room temperature. *Makes one 9×5-inch loaf*

GINGERBREAD SCONES WITH LEMON BREAKFAST CREAM

¼ cup sugar, divided
1¾ cups all-purpose flour
¾ cup QUAKER® Oats (quick or old fashioned, uncooked)
4 teaspoons baking powder
1 teaspoon ground ginger
½ teaspoon ground cinnamon
¼ teaspoon ground nutmeg
⅛ teaspoon ground cloves
⅓ cup (5⅓ tablespoons) margarine
⅓ cup skim milk
⅓ cup dried currants or raisins
2 egg whites, slightly beaten
2 tablespoons molasses

LEMON BREAKFAST CREAM

¾ cup part-skim ricotta cheese
2 tablespoons frozen lemonade concentrate, thawed

Preheat oven to 425°F. Reserve 1 teaspoon of sugar. Combine remaining sugar with flour, oats, baking powder, ginger, cinnamon, nutmeg and cloves; mix well. Cut in margarine until crumbly. Combine milk, currants, egg whites and molasses. Add to flour mixture, mixing just until moistened. Turn out onto lightly floured surface; knead gently 5 to 10 times. Pat dough to ¾-inch thickness. Cut with 2½-inch heart-shaped or round biscuit cutter. Place on ungreased cookie sheet. Sprinkle tops with reserved 1 teaspoon sugar. Bake 9 to 11 minutes or until golden brown.

Place ricotta cheese and lemonade concentrate in food processor or blender; process until smooth. Serve with warm scones. *Makes 10 scones*

VARIATION: For thinner consistency Lemon Breakfast Cream, add ½ cup low fat lemon yogurt.

Gingerbread Scones with Lemon Breakfast Cream

CRANBERRY RAISIN NUT BREAD

1½ cups all-purpose flour
¾ cup packed light brown sugar
1½ teaspoons baking powder
½ teaspoon baking soda
½ teaspoon ground cinnamon
½ teaspoon ground nutmeg
1 cup halved fresh or frozen cranberries
½ cup golden raisins
½ cup coarsely chopped pecans
1 tablespoon grated orange peel
2 eggs
¾ cup milk
3 tablespoons butter or margarine, melted
1 teaspoon vanilla
Cranberry-Orange Spread (recipe follows), optional

Preheat oven to 350°F. Grease 8½×4½-inch loaf pan.

Combine flour, brown sugar, baking powder, baking soda, cinnamon and nutmeg in large bowl. Stir in cranberries, raisins, pecans and orange peel. Mix eggs, milk, melted butter and vanilla in small bowl until combined; stir into flour mixture just until moistened. Spoon into prepared pan.

Bake 55 to 60 minutes until wooden pick inserted in center comes out clean. Cool in pan 15 minutes. Remove from pan and cool completely on wire rack. Store tightly wrapped in plastic wrap at room temperature. Serve slices with Cranberry-Orange Spread, if desired. *Makes one 8½×4½-inch loaf*

Cranberry-Orange Spread

1 package (8 ounces) cream cheese, softened
1 package (3 ounces) cream cheese, softened
1 container (12 ounces) cranberry-orange sauce
¾ cup chopped pecans

Combine cream cheese and cranberry-orange sauce in small bowl. Stir with spoon until blended. Stir in pecans. Store refrigerated.
Makes about 3 cups spread

Cranberry Raisin Nut Bread

WHOLE WHEAT HERBED BREAD WREATH

- **4 cups all-purpose flour, divided**
- **2 packages active dry yeast**
- **2 tablespoons sugar**
- **4 teaspoons dried rosemary leaves**
- **1 tablespoon salt**
- **2½ cups water**
- **2 tablespoons olive oil**
- **3 cups whole wheat flour, divided**
- **1 egg, beaten**

Combine 2½ cups all-purpose flour, yeast, sugar, rosemary and salt in large bowl. Heat water until very warm (120° to 130°F). Gradually add to flour mixture with oil until blended. Beat with electric mixer at medium speed 2 minutes. Add 1 cup whole wheat flour. Beat at high speed 2 minutes, scraping side of bowl occasionally. By hand, stir in enough of remaining flours to make a soft, sticky dough. Place in greased bowl; turn to grease top of dough. Cover with towel. Let rise in warm place about 1½ hours or until doubled in bulk.

Punch down dough. Turn out onto well-floured surface. Knead about 10 minutes or until smooth and elastic. Divide into thirds. Roll each piece to form 24-inch rope. Place on large greased cookie sheet. Braid ropes beginning at center and working toward both ends. Seal ends together. Shape into circle around greased 10-ounce ovenproof round bowl. Seal ends well. Cover with towel. Let rise in warm place about 30 minutes or until doubled in bulk.

Preheat oven to 450°F. Carefully brush wreath with egg. Bake 25 to 30 minutes or until wreath sounds hollow when tapped and top is golden brown. Cool on cookie sheet 10 minutes. Carefully remove from cookie sheet and bowl; cool completely on wire rack. Store tightly wrapped in plastic wrap at room temperature.

Makes one 12-inch wreath

Whole Wheat Herbed Bread Wreath

SPICY CHEESE BREAD

2 envelopes active dry yeast
1 teaspoon granulated sugar
½ cup warm water (110°F)
8½ cups all-purpose flour, divided
3 cups (12 ounces) shredded Jarlsberg or Swiss cheese
2 tablespoons fresh chopped rosemary *or* 2 teaspoons dried rosemary
1 tablespoon salt
1 tablespoon TABASCO® pepper sauce
2 cups milk
4 eggs

In small bowl, stir yeast, sugar and warm water; let stand 5 minutes until foamy.

Meanwhile, in large bowl combine 8 cups flour, cheese, rosemary, salt and TABASCO sauce. In small saucepan over low heat, heat milk until warm (120° to 130°F). Stir into flour mixture. In medium bowl, lightly beat eggs; set aside 1 tablespoon beaten egg. Add remaining eggs to flour mixture along with yeast mixture; stir until mixture forms a soft dough.

On lightly floured surface, knead dough 5 minutes or until smooth and elastic, kneading in remaining ½ cup flour. Shape dough into a ball and place in large greased bowl, turning dough over to grease top. Cover with towel and let rise in warm place until doubled, about 1½ hours.

Grease two large cookie sheets. Punch down dough and divide in half. Cut each half into 3 strips and braid. Place each braid on cookie sheet. Cover and let rise in warm place until almost doubled, 30 minutes to 1 hour.

Preheat oven to 375°F. Brush braids with reserved 1 tablespoon beaten egg. Bake about 45 minutes or until braids sound hollow when lightly tapped. Remove to wire racks to cool. *Makes 2 braids*

BEST EVER BLUEBERRY STREUSEL MUFFINS

Streusel Topping (page 31)
2 cups all-purpose flour
1 cup JACK FROST® granulated sugar
4 teaspoons baking powder
1 teaspoon baking soda
¼ teaspoon salt
1 cup buttermilk
1 egg, beaten
¼ cup butter, melted
1 teaspoon vanilla
1 cup frozen blueberries, slightly thawed*
1 tablespoon all-purpose flour

*Fresh blueberries can be used.

Preheat oven to 400°F. Prepare Streusel Topping; set aside. Combine 2 cups flour, sugar, baking powder, baking soda and salt in large bowl; set aside. Combine buttermilk, egg, butter and vanilla in small bowl. Add liquid ingredients to dry ingredients all at once, stirring until flour is moistened (batter will be lumpy). Stir together blueberries and 1 tablespoon flour in small bowl

until blueberries are coated; fold into batter. Fill paper-lined muffin tins ¾ full. Sprinkle about 1 tablespoon Streusel Topping on each muffin. Bake 20 minutes (30 minutes for jumbo).

Makes 12 or 14 medium muffins or 6 jumbo muffins

Streusel Topping

3 tablespoons all-purpose flour
2 tablespoons JACK FROST® granulated sugar
¼ teaspoon ground cinnamon
1 tablespoon butter, melted
¼ cup sliced almonds

Combine flour, sugar and cinnamon in small bowl. Using fork, stir in butter until mixture forms coarse crumbs. Stir in sliced almonds.

FESTIVE YULE LOAF

2¾ cups all-purpose flour, divided
⅓ cup sugar
1 teaspoon salt
1 package active dry yeast
1 cup milk
½ cup butter or margarine
1 egg
½ cup golden raisins
½ cup chopped candied red and green cherries
½ cup chopped pecans
Vanilla Glaze (recipe follows), optional

Combine 1½ cups flour, sugar, salt and yeast in large bowl. Heat milk and butter over medium heat until very warm (120° to 130°F). Gradually stir into flour mixture. Add egg. Mix with electric mixer at low speed 1 minute. Beat at high speed 3 minutes, scraping side of bowl frequently. Toss raisins, cherries and pecans with ¼ cup flour in small bowl; stir into yeast mixture. Stir in enough of remaining 1 cup flour to make a soft dough. Turn out onto lightly floured surface. Knead about 10 minutes or until smooth and elastic. Place in greased bowl; turn to grease top of dough. Cover with towel. Let rise in warm place about 1 hour or until doubled in bulk.

Punch down dough. Divide in half. Roll out each half on lightly floured surface to form 8-inch circle. Fold in half; press only folded edge firmly. Place on ungreased cookie sheet. Cover with towel. Let rise in warm place about 30 minutes or until doubled in bulk.

Preheat oven to 375°F. Bake 20 to 25 minutes until golden brown. Remove from cookie sheet and cool completely on wire rack. Frost with Vanilla Glaze, if desired. Store in airtight containers.

Makes 2 loaves

VANILLA GLAZE: Combine 1 cup sifted powdered sugar, 4 to 5 teaspoons light cream or half-and-half and ½ teaspoon vanilla extract in small bowl; stir until smooth.

WALNUT CHEDDAR APPLE BREAD

½ cup butter or margarine, softened
1 cup packed light brown sugar
2 eggs
1 teaspoon vanilla
2 cups all-purpose flour
2 teaspoons baking powder
1 teaspoon baking soda
¼ teaspoon salt
1 cup dairy sour cream
¼ cup milk
1 cup (4 ounces) shredded Cheddar cheese
1 cup diced dried apple
½ cup coarsely chopped walnuts

Preheat oven to 350°F. Grease 9×5-inch loaf pan.

Beat butter and sugar in large bowl with electric mixer at medium speed until light and fluffy. Beat in eggs and vanilla until blended. Combine flour, baking powder, baking soda and salt in small bowl. Add flour mixture to butter mixture alternately with sour cream and milk, beginning and ending with flour mixture; beat well at low speed after each addition. Stir in cheese, apple and walnuts until blended. Spoon into prepared pan.

Bake 50 to 55 minutes or until wooden pick inserted in center comes out clean. Cool in pan 15 minutes. Remove from pan and cool completely on wire rack. Store tightly wrapped in plastic wrap at room temperature. *Makes one 9×5-inch loaf*

SPICY GINGERBREAD WITH CINNAMON PEAR SAUCE

2 cups all-purpose flour
½ cup packed light brown sugar
1 teaspoon baking soda
1 teaspoon ground ginger
1 teaspoon ground cinnamon
¼ teaspoon ground cloves
¼ teaspoon salt
1 cup light molasses
¾ cup buttermilk
½ cup butter or margarine, softened
Cinnamon Pear Sauce (page 34)

Preheat oven to 325°F. Grease and lightly flour 9-inch square baking pan.

Combine all ingredients except Cinnamon Pear Sauce in large bowl. Beat with electric mixer at low speed until well blended, scraping side of bowl with rubber spatula frequently. Beat at high speed 2 minutes more. Pour into prepared pan.

Bake 50 to 55 minutes until wooden pick inserted in center comes out clean. Cool in pan on wire rack about 30 minutes. Cut into squares; serve warm with Cinnamon Pear Sauce.

Makes 9 servings

continued

Walnut Cheddar Apple Bread

Cinnamon Pear Sauce

- **2 cans (16 ounces each) pear halves in syrup, undrained**
- **2 tablespoons sugar**
- **1 teaspoon fresh lemon juice**
- **½ teaspoon ground cinnamon**

Drain pear halves, reserving ¼ cup syrup. Place pears, reserved syrup, sugar, lemon juice and cinnamon in work bowl of food processor or blender; cover. Process until smooth. Just before serving, place pear sauce in medium saucepan; heat until warm. *Makes 2 cups sauce*

SWEET AND SPICY FRUITCAKE

- **3 cups chopped walnuts**
- **2 cups chopped dried figs**
- **1 cup chopped dried apricots**
- **1 cup chocolate chips**
- **1½ cups all-purpose flour, divided**
- **¾ cup sugar**
- **4 large eggs**
- **¼ cup butter or margarine, softened**
- **⅓ cup apple jelly***
- **2 tablespoons orange-flavored liqueur**
- **1 tablespoon grated orange peel**
- **1 tablespoon vanilla**
- **2 teaspoons TABASCO® pepper sauce**
- **1 teaspoon baking powder**

*Or, substitute ⅓ cup McIlhenny Farms™ Pepper Jelly for apple jelly and omit TABASCO® pepper sauce.

Preheat oven to 325°F. Grease two 3-cup ovenproof bowls. Line bottoms and sides with foil; grease foil. In large bowl, combine walnuts, figs, apricots, chocolate chips and ¼ cup flour; set aside.

In small bowl with electric mixer at low speed, beat sugar, eggs and butter until well blended. Add jelly, remaining 1¼ cups flour and remaining ingredients. Beat at low speed until blended. Toss mixture with dried fruit in large bowl. Spoon into prepared bowls. Cover bowls with greased foil. Bake 40 minutes; uncover and bake 40 minutes longer or until wooden toothpick inserted in centers comes out clean. Remove to wire racks to cool.

If desired, brush cooled fruitcakes with 1 tablespoon melted apple jelly and sprinkle each with 2 tablespoons finely chopped dried apricots. Store in cool place up to 3 weeks.

Makes 2 small fruitcakes

Top to bottom: *Spicy Cheese Bread (page 30) and Sweet and Spicy Fruitcake*

TO:
FROM:

Holiday Pumpkin-Nut Muffins

2½ cups all-purpose flour
1 cup packed light brown sugar
1 tablespoon baking powder
1 teaspoon ground cinnamon
½ teaspoon ground nutmeg
½ teaspoon ground ginger
¼ teaspoon salt
1 cup canned pumpkin
¾ cup milk
2 eggs
6 tablespoons butter or margarine, melted
⅔ cup roasted, salted pepitas (pumpkin seeds), divided
½ cup golden raisins

Preheat oven to 400°F. Grease or paper-line 18 (2¾-inch) muffin cups.

Combine flour, brown sugar, baking powder, cinnamon, nutmeg, ginger and salt in large bowl. Stir pumpkin, milk, eggs and butter in medium bowl until well blended. Stir pumpkin mixture into flour mixture. Mix *just* until all ingredients are moistened. Stir in ⅓ cup pepitas and raisins. Spoon into prepared muffin cups, filling ⅔ full. Sprinkle remaining pepitas over muffin batter.

Bake 15 to 18 minutes until wooden pick inserted in center comes out clean. Cool in pans 10 minutes. Remove from pans and cool completely on wire racks. Store in airtight container.

Makes 18 (2¾-inch) muffins

Spicy Mincemeat Bread

6 tablespoons butter or margarine
1 cup packed light brown sugar
2 eggs
1 teaspoon vanilla
2½ cups all-purpose flour
1½ teaspoons baking soda
1 teaspoon ground cinnamon
¾ teaspoon baking powder
½ teaspoon ground nutmeg
¼ teaspoon salt
¾ cup dairy sour cream
1 cup prepared mincemeat
¾ cup chopped pecans

Preheat oven to 350°F. Grease 9×5-inch loaf pan.

Beat butter and brown sugar in large bowl with electric mixer at medium speed until light and fluffy. Beat in eggs and vanilla until blended. Combine flour, baking soda, cinnamon, baking powder, nutmeg and salt. Add flour mixture to butter mixture alternately with sour cream, beginning and ending with flour mixture; beat at low speed after each addition. Stir in mincemeat and pecans until blended. Spoon into prepared pan.

Bake 55 to 60 minutes until wooden pick inserted in center comes out clean. Cool in pan 15 minutes. Remove from pan and cool completely on wire rack. Store tightly wrapped in plastic wrap at room temperature.

Makes one 9×5-inch loaf

Holiday Pumpkin-Nut Muffins

SPICED BANANA AND RAISIN LOAVES

3¼ cups all-purpose flour
¼ cup toasted wheat germ
1 tablespoon baking powder
2 teaspoons ground cinnamon
2 teaspoons ground ginger
1 teaspoon salt
1 teaspoon ground nutmeg
½ teaspoon baking soda
1½ cups butter or margarine
1⅓ cups sugar
4 eggs
4 ripe bananas
¼ cup milk
2 boxes (15 ounces each) golden raisins
1 can (6 ounces) walnuts or pecans, coarsely chopped
Light corn syrup
Candied fruit

Preheat oven to 325°F. Grease and flour six 5¼×3¼-inch loaf pans.* Combine flour, wheat germ, baking powder, cinnamon, ginger, salt, nutmeg and baking soda in large bowl; set aside. Beat butter and sugar in large bowl with electric mixer at medium speed until light and fluffy. Add eggs, one at a time, beating well after each. Place bananas and milk in food processor or blender; process until smooth. Alternately add flour and banana mixtures to butter and egg mixture; beat just until blended. Stir in raisins and walnuts. Spoon into prepared pans; spread smooth. Bake about 45 minutes or until wooden pick inserted in center comes out clean. Cool in pans on wire rack 10 minutes. Remove from pans and cool completely on wire rack. Wrap securely and freeze until ready to serve. To decorate, brush tops with light corn syrup. Arrange candied fruit over tops.

Makes 6 small loaf cakes or 2 large loaf cakes

*Loaves may also be baked in two 9×5-inch greased and floured loaf pans. Prepare as directed. Bake at 325°F for 1 hour or until wooden pick inserted in center comes out clean. Proceed as directed.

Favorite recipe from ***American Spice Trade Association***

Top to bottom: *Tiny Spiced Cakes (page 104) and Spiced Banana and Raisin Loaves*

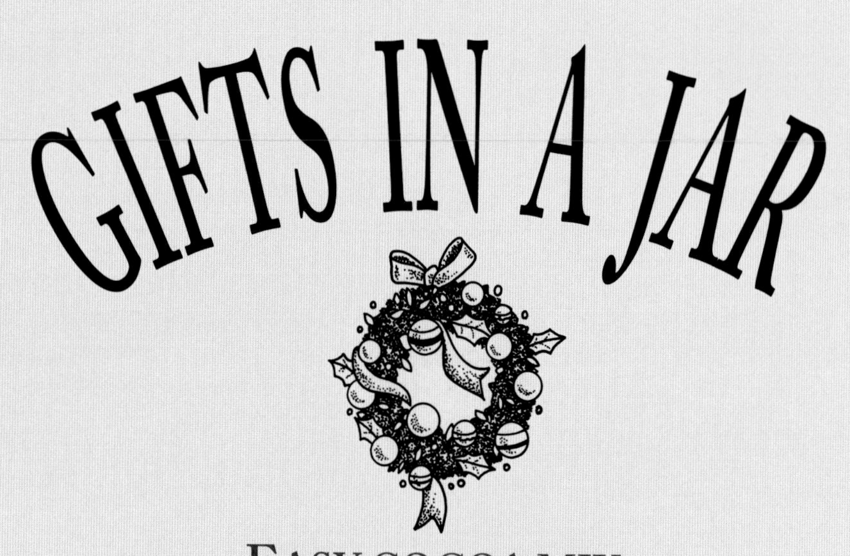

EASY COCOA MIX

2 cups nonfat dry milk powder
1 cup sugar
¾ cup powdered non-dairy creamer
½ cup unsweetened cocoa
¼ teaspoon salt

Combine all ingredients in 1-quart airtight container or decorative gift jar; cover.

Makes about 4 cups mix or 16 servings

FOR SINGLE SERVING: Place rounded ¼ cup Easy Cocoa Mix in mug or cup; add ¾ cup boiling water. Stir until mix is dissolved. Top with sweetened whipped cream and marshmallows, if desired. Serve immediately.

COCOA MARSHMALLOW MIX: Prepare Easy Cocoa Mix in 2-quart airtight container as directed adding 1 package (10½ ounces) miniature marshmallows.

Makes about 7 cups mix or 14 servings

FOR SINGLE SERVING: Place rounded ½ cup Cocoa Marshmallow Mix in mug or cup; add ¾ cup boiling water. Stir until mix is dissolved. Serve immediately.

Left to right: *Easy Cocoa Mix and Mocha Coffee Mix (page 52)*

RICH CHOCOLATE SAUCE

1 cup whipping cream
⅓ cup light corn syrup
1 cup (6 ounces) semisweet chocolate chips
1 to 2 tablespoons dark rum (optional)
1 teaspoon vanilla

Place cream and corn syrup in heavy 2-quart saucepan. Stir over medium heat until mixture boils. Remove from heat. Stir in chocolate, rum, if desired, and vanilla until chocolate is melted. Cool 10 minutes. Serve warm or pour into clean glass jars and seal tightly. Store up to 6 months in refrigerator. Reheat sauce over low heat before serving. *Makes about 1¾ cups sauce*

CREAMY CARAMEL SAUCE

1 cup granulated sugar
1 cup whipping cream
½ cup packed light brown sugar
⅓ cup corn syrup
1 teaspoon vanilla

Place granulated sugar, cream, brown sugar and corn syrup in heavy 2-quart saucepan. Stir over low heat until mixture boils. Carefully clip candy thermometer to side of pan (do not let bulb touch bottom of pan). Cook, stirring occasionally, about 20 minutes or until thermometer registers 238°F. Immediately remove from heat. Stir in vanilla. Cool about 15 minutes. Serve warm or pour into clean glass jars and seal tightly. Store up to 6 months in refrigerator. Reheat sauce over low heat before serving. *Makes about 2 cups sauce*

GOOEY HOT FUDGE SAUCE

2 cups (12 ounces) semisweet chocolate chips
2 tablespoons butter
½ cup half-and-half
1 tablespoon corn syrup
⅛ teaspoon salt
½ teaspoon vanilla

Melt chocolate and butter with half-and-half, corn syrup and salt in heavy 2-quart saucepan over low heat, stirring until smooth. Remove from heat; let stand 10 minutes. Stir in vanilla. Serve warm or pour into clean glass jars and seal tightly. Store up to 6 months in refrigerator. Reheat sauce in double-boiler over hot (not boiling) water before serving, if desired. *Makes about 1½ cups sauce*

Clockwise from top left: *Spicy Cocktail Sauce (page 18), Gooey Hot Fudge Sauce, Rich Chocolate Sauce and Creamy Caramel Sauce*

HOLIDAY APPLE CHUTNEY

- 9 (½-pint) jelly jars with lids and screw bands
- 8 large tart apples, peeled, cored and chopped (about 4 pounds)
- 2 large onions, chopped
- 2 cups golden raisins
- 1 package (16 ounces) packed brown sugar (2¼ cups)
- 2 cups granulated sugar
- 1 cup cider vinegar
- Grated peel and juice of 2 oranges and 1 lemon
- 2 tablespoons finely chopped crystallized ginger
- 2 teaspoons ground cinnamon
- ½ teaspoon ground cloves

Wash jars, lids and bands. Leave jars in hot water. Place lids and bands in large pan of water.

Combine remaining ingredients in heavy 8-quart saucepan or Dutch oven. Bring to a boil over high heat. Reduce heat to medium-low. Simmer, uncovered, 30 minutes or until mixture thickens, stirring frequently.

Bring water with lids and bands to a boil. Ladle hot mixture into hot jars leaving ½-inch space at top. Run metal spatula around inside of jar to remove air bubbles. Wipe tops and sides of jar rims clean. Place hot lids and bands on jar. Screw bands tightly, but do not force. To process, place jars in boiling water; boil 10 minutes. Remove jars with tongs; cool on wire racks. (Check seals by pressing on lid with fingertip; lid should remain concave.) Label and date jars. Store unopened jars in a cool, dry place up to 12 months. Refrigerate after opening up to 6 months.

Makes about nine ½-pint jars

TRIPLE TREAT SAUCE

- 2 cups (12-ounce package) NESTLÉ® TOLL HOUSE® Semi-Sweet Chocolate Morsels
- 2 cups (12-ounce package) NESTLÉ® TOLL HOUSE® Butterscotch Flavored Morsels
- 1 cup smooth peanut butter
- 1½ cups (12 fluid-ounce can) undiluted CARNATION® Evaporated Milk
- ½ cup coarsely chopped dry roasted peanuts

MELT chocolate morsels, butterscotch morsels and peanut butter in medium, heavy saucepan over low heat, stirring constantly until almost smooth. Remove from heat; whisk in milk. Stir in peanuts.

SERVE warm over ice cream or cake; chill remaining sauce. *Makes about 4½ cups sauce*

Crock of Spice for Apple Cider

12 cinnamon sticks, broken into small pieces
¼ cup whole cloves
¼ cup allspice berries
¼ cup juniper berries
1 tablespoon dried orange peel, chopped
1 tablespoon dried lemon peel, chopped
1 teaspoon ground nutmeg

Combine all ingredients in airtight container. To prepare spiced cider, measure 1 heaping teaspoon spice mixture for each mug of cider into large saucepan. Simmer cider with spices 5 minutes. Strain before serving.

VARIATION: Pack into small bags you have made from Christmas fabrics or into muslin bouquet garni bags available at kitchen or specialty stores. Use like tea bags to flavor mugs of hot cider or mulled wine.

GIFT TIP: Put mixture in crock or attractive container and give with jug of country apple cider from your favorite farm stand or market. Include instructions for making spiced cider on a recipe card with the gift.

Tarragon Chive Vinegar

4 to 5 sprigs fresh tarragon
⅓ cup snipped fresh chives
1 bottle (16 ounces) HEINZ® Apple Cider or Distilled White Vinegar
Fresh tarragon sprigs, for garnish
Fresh chives, for garnish

Lightly bruise tarragon sprigs; place in sterilized pint jar with chives. Heat vinegar to just below the boiling point. Fill jar with vinegar and cap tightly. Allow to stand 3 to 4 weeks. Strain vinegar, discarding herbs. Pour vinegar into clean sterilized jar, adding fresh tarragon sprigs and chives for garnish, if desired. Seal tightly. Use in marinades for mushrooms or artichokes, or in dressings for tossed green or pasta salads.

Makes 2 cups vinegar

Raspberry Vinaigrette

½ cup vegetable oil
½ cup raspberry vinegar
2 teaspoons Dijon mustard
½ to 1 teaspoon sugar
¼ teaspoon black pepper

Combine all ingredients in jar with tight-fitting lid; shake vigorously. Refrigerate to blend flavors. Shake again before serving with mixed green salads.

Makes about 1 cup vinaigrette

Favorite recipe from ***Heinz U.S.A.***

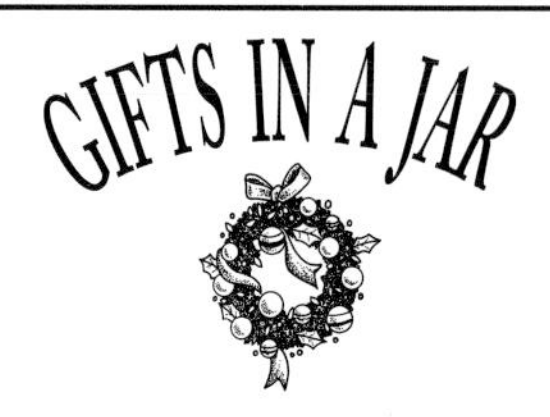

HOT CHOCOLATE FUDGE SAUCE

- **¾ cup sugar**
- **¾ cup heavy or whipping cream**
- **½ cup KARO® Light Corn Syrup**
- **2 tablespoons MAZOLA® margarine or butter**
- **1 package (8 ounces) semisweet chocolate**
- **1 teaspoon vanilla**

In large saucepan, combine sugar, cream, corn syrup and margarine. Stirring constantly, bring to a full boil over medium heat. Remove from heat. Stir in chocolate until melted. Stir in vanilla. Serve warm over ice cream. Store in refrigerator.

Makes about 2¼ cups

Prep Time: 10 minutes, plus cooling

EVER-SO-GOOD PEANUT BUTTER SAUCE

- **½ cup KARO® Light or Dark Corn Syrup**
- **½ cup SKIPPY® Super Chunk or creamy peanut butter**
- **3 to 4 tablespoons milk**

In small bowl, stir corn syrup, peanut butter and milk until blended. Serve over ice cream or cake. Store in refrigerator. *Makes about 1¼ cups sauce*

Prep Time: 5 minutes

MAPLE WALNUT RAISIN SAUCE

- **1 cup KARO® Light or Dark Corn Syrup**
- **½ cup packed brown sugar**
- **½ cup heavy or whipping cream**
- **½ cup coarsely chopped walnuts**
- **¼ cup raisins**
- **½ teaspoon maple-flavored extract**

In medium saucepan, combine corn syrup, brown sugar and cream. Stirring constantly, bring to a full boil over medium heat and boil 1 minute. Remove from heat. Stir in walnuts, raisins and maple extract. Serve warm. Store in refrigerator.

Makes 2 cups sauce

Prep Time: 10 minutes

Top to bottom: *Hot Chocolate Fudge Sauce, Ever-So-Good Peanut Butter Sauce and Maple Walnut Raisin Sauce*

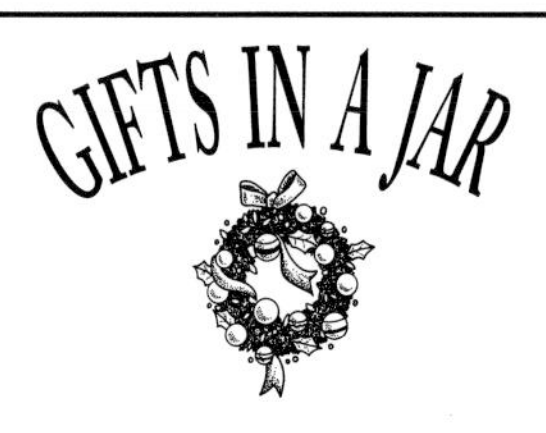

CHRISTMAS CITRUS MARMALADE

2 lemons
1 orange
2½ cups water
⅛ teaspoon baking soda
1 large grapefruit
7 (½-pint) jelly jars with lids and screw bands
1 box (1¾ ounces) powdered fruit pectin
6 cups sugar

Remove peel from white part of lemons and orange in long strips with sharp paring knife, making sure there is no white pith on the peel. Stack strips; cut into thin slivers. Combine lemon and orange peels, water and baking soda in 2-quart saucepan. Bring to a boil over high heat. Reduce heat to low; cover and simmer 20 minutes, stirring occasionally.

Meanwhile, peel grapefruit. Remove white pith from grapefruit, lemons and orange; discard peel and pith. Separate fruit into sections. With fingers, remove pulp from membrane of each section over saucepan to save juice. Dice fruit sections into same saucepan. Bring to a boil. Cover and simmer 10 minutes. Measure 5 cups fruit mixture into 6-quart saucepan or Dutch oven.

Wash jars, lids and bands. Leave jars in hot water. Place lids and bands in large pan of water. Mix pectin into fruit mixture. Bring to a rolling boil over medium-high heat, stirring constantly. Immediately stir in sugar. Bring to a rolling boil and boil 1 minute, stirring constantly. Remove from heat; skim off foam with metal spoon.

Bring water with lids and bands to a boil. Ladle hot mixture into hot jars leaving ½-inch space at top. Run metal spatula around inside of jar to remove air bubbles. Wipe tops and sides of jar rims clean. Place hot lids and bands on jar. Screw bands tightly, but do not force. To process, place jars in boiling water; boil 10 minutes. Remove jars with tongs; cool on wire racks. (Check seals by pressing on lid with fingertip; lid should remain concave.) Label and date jars.* Store unopened jars in a cool, dry place up to 12 months. Refrigerate after opening up to 6 months.

Makes about seven ½-pint jars

*Marmalade sets slowly. Store in a cool, dry place 2 weeks before serving.

Clockwise from top: *Cranberry-Orange Relish (page 54), Freezer Plum Conserve (page 54) and Christmas Citrus Marmalade*

SPICY RED PEPPER JELLY

2 large red bell peppers, coarsely chopped (about 4 cups)
1 small onion, cut into wedges (about 1 cup)
1½ cups apple cider vinegar, divided
6½ cups sugar
1 (3-ounce) pouch liquid pectin
3 to 4 teaspoons TABASCO® pepper sauce

Place bell peppers, onion and ¼ cup vinegar in food processor; process until very finely ground. Transfer mixture to large, heavy nonaluminum saucepan. Add remaining 1¼ cups vinegar; bring to a full boil over high heat. Reduce heat to low; simmer 5 minutes, stirring occasionally, until mixture is slightly thickened. Stir in sugar; increase heat to high and bring to a full rolling boil, stirring constantly. Boil 1 minute, stirring constantly. (Be careful; jam has a tendency to boil over and is very hot. Adjust heat if necessary.) Remove from heat. Stir in pectin; mix until completely blended. Skim off foam that rises to surface. Stir in TABASCO sauce to taste. Ladle jam into hot sterilized jars (½-pint size are ideal), leaving ¼-inch headspace. Wipe inside and outside rims clean with damp paper towel. Seal with sterilized new 2-piece lids, following manufacturer's instructions. Cool jars on wire rack. Store in cool place up to 6 months. Refrigerate after opening.

Makes 7 cups jelly

CHUNKY SALSA

2 tablespoons olive oil
1 cup coarsely chopped onion
1 cup coarsely diced green bell pepper
1 can (35 ounces) tomatoes, drained and coarsely chopped (reserve ½ cup juice)
1 tablespoon freshly squeezed lime juice
2 teaspoons TABASCO® pepper sauce
½ teaspoon salt
2 tablespoons chopped fresh cilantro or Italian parsley

Heat oil in large, heavy saucepan over high heat. Add onion and bell pepper; sauté 5 to 6 minutes, stirring frequently, until tender. Add tomatoes with reserved ½ cup juice; bring to a boil over high heat. Reduce heat to low and simmer 6 to 8 minutes, stirring occasionally, until salsa is slightly thickened. Remove from heat. Stir in lime juice, TABASCO sauce to taste and salt. Cool to lukewarm; stir in cilantro. Spoon salsa into clean jars. Keep refrigerated for up to 5 days.

Makes 3½ cups

***Top to bottom:** Spicy Red Pepper Jelly and Chunky Salsa*

GIFTS IN A JAR

HERBED VINEGAR

- 1 bottle (12 ounces) white wine vinegar (1½ cups)
- ½ cup fresh basil leaves

Pour vinegar into nonaluminum 2-quart saucepan. Heat until very hot, stirring occasionally. *Do not boil.* (If vinegar boils, it will become cloudy.)

Pour into glass bowl; add basil. Cover with plastic wrap. Let stand in cool place about 1 week until desired amount of flavor develops. Strain before using. Store up to 6 months in jar or bottle with tight-fitting lid. *Makes about 1½ cups vinegar*

VARIATIONS: Substitute 1 tablespoon of either fresh oregano, thyme, chervil or tarragon for the basil. Or, substitute cider vinegar for the wine vinegar.

RASPBERRY VINEGAR

- 1 bottle (12 ounces) white wine vinegar (1½ cups)
- ½ cup sugar
- 1 cup fresh raspberries or sliced strawberries, crushed

Combine vinegar and sugar in nonaluminum 2-quart saucepan. Heat until very hot, stirring occasionally. *Do not boil.* (If vinegar boils, it will become cloudy.)

Pour into glass bowl; stir in raspberries. Cover with plastic wrap. Let stand in cool place about 1 week until desired amount of flavor develops. Strain through fine-mesh sieve or cheesecloth twice. Store up to 6 months in jar or bottle with tight-fitting lid in refrigerator.

Makes about 2 cups vinegar

MOCHA COFFEE MIX

- 1 cup nonfat dry milk powder
- ¾ cup granulated sugar
- ⅔ cup powdered non-dairy creamer
- ½ cup unsweetened cocoa
- ⅓ cup instant coffee, pressed through fine sieve
- ¼ cup packed brown sugar
- 1 teaspoon ground cinnamon
- ¼ teaspoon salt
- ¼ teaspoon ground nutmeg

Combine all ingredients in 1-quart airtight container or decorative gift jar; cover.

Makes about 3¼ cups mix or 10 to 12 servings

FOR SINGLE SERVING: Place rounded ¼ cup Mocha Coffee Mix in mug or cup; add ¾ cup boiling water. Stir until mix is dissolved. Serve immediately.

Left to right: *Herbed Vinegar and Raspberry Vinegar*

FREEZER PLUM CONSERVE

4 (½-pint) jelly jars with lids
2 cans (16 ounces each) whole purple plums, drained and pitted
1 tablespoon grated orange peel
1 large orange, peeled and sectioned
4 cups sugar
1 cup raisins
½ cup chopped walnuts
¾ cup water
1 box (1¾ ounces) powdered fruit pectin

Rinse clean jars and lids with boiling water.

Place plums, orange peel and orange sections in food processor or blender; process until plums are chopped. Measure 2 cups mixture into large bowl. Stir sugar into plum mixture until well blended. Stir in raisins and walnuts. Let stand 10 minutes, stirring occasionally. Mix water and pectin in 1-quart saucepan. (Mixture may be lumpy.) Bring to a boil over high heat, stirring constantly. Boil and stir 1 minute. Stir hot pectin mixture into fruit mixture. Stir constantly for 3 minutes.

Ladle hot mixture into jars leaving ½-inch space at top. Run metal spatula around inside of jar to remove air bubbles. Wipe tops and sides of jar rims clean; quickly cover with lids. Let stand at room temperature up to 24 hours or until set. Store in freezer up to 12 months. Thaw jars in refrigerator overnight before using. Refrigerate after opening up to 6 months. *Makes about four ½-pint jars*

CRANBERRY-ORANGE RELISH

4 large oranges, divided
7 (½-pint) jelly jars with lids and screw bands
2 cups sugar
½ cup water
2 packages (12 ounces each) fresh cranberries, washed and drained

Remove peel from white part of 2 oranges in long strips with sharp paring knife, making sure there is no white pith on the peel. Stack strips; cut into thin slivers. Measure ¼ cup.

Add orange peel to 1 inch boiling water in 1-quart saucepan. Boil over medium heat 5 minutes. Drain and set aside. Peel remaining 2 oranges and remove white pith from all 4 oranges; discard peel and pith. Separate oranges into sections. With fingers, remove pulp from membrane of each section over 2-cup measure to save juice. Dice orange sections into same cup measure. Add additional water to orange mixture to make 2 cups, if necessary.

Wash jars, lids and bands. Leave jars in hot water. Place lids and bands in large pan of water.

Combine sugar and water in heavy 6-quart saucepan or Dutch oven. Bring to a boil over medium heat. Add reserved orange peel, orange mixture and cranberries. Bring to a boil, stirring occasionally. Boil about 10 minutes or until mixture thickens gently and cranberries pop.

GIFTS IN A JAR

Bring water with lids and bands to a boil. Ladle hot mixture into hot jars leaving ½-inch space at top. Run metal spatula around inside of jar to remove air bubbles. Wipe tops and sides of jar rims clean. Place hot lids and bands on jar. Screw bands tightly, but do not force. To process, place jars in boiling water; boil 10 minutes. Remove jars with tongs; cool on wire racks. (Check seals by pressing on lid with fingertip; lid should remain concave.) Label and date jars. Store unopened jars in a cool, dry place up to 12 months. Refrigerate after opening up to 6 months.

Makes about seven ½-pint jars

BASIL GARLIC VINEGAR

½ cup coarsely chopped fresh basil leaves
2 cloves garlic, peeled and split
1 bottle (16 ounces) HEINZ® Wine or Distilled White Vinegar
Fresh basil leaves, for garnish

Place basil and garlic in sterilized pint jar. Heat vinegar to just below boiling point. Fill jar with vinegar and cap tightly. Allow to stand 3 to 4 weeks. Strain vinegar, discarding basil and garlic. Pour vinegar into clean sterilized jar, adding fresh basil for garnish, if desired. Seal tightly. Use in dressings for rice, pasta, antipasto salads or in flavored mayonnaise. *Makes 2 cups vinegar*

SPICY GERMAN MUSTARD

½ cup mustard seeds
2 tablespoons dry mustard
½ cup cold water
1 cup cider vinegar
1 small onion, chopped
2 cloves garlic, minced
3 tablespoons packed brown sugar
¾ teaspoon salt
¼ teaspoon dried tarragon leaves
¼ teaspoon ground cinnamon

Combine mustard seeds, dry mustard and water in small bowl. Cover; let stand at least 4 hours or overnight.

Combine vinegar, onion, garlic, brown sugar, salt, tarragon and cinnamon in noncorrosive heavy 1-quart saucepan. Bring to a boil over high heat; reduce heat to medium. Boil, uncovered, about 7 to 10 minutes until mixture is reduced by half.

Pour vinegar mixture through fine sieve into food processor bowl. Rinse saucepan; set aside. Add mustard mixture to vinegar mixture; process about 1 minute or until mustard seeds are chopped but not puréed. Pour into same saucepan. Cook over low heat until mustard is thick, stirring constantly. Store in airtight container or decorative gift jars up to 1 year in refrigerator. *Makes about 1 cup*

PEPPERCORN COOKIES

1 cup all-purpose flour
⅔ cup plus 1 tablespoon sugar, divided
1 teaspoon baking powder
½ teaspoon ground black pepper
Pinch ground red pepper
½ cup (1 stick) butter, melted
1 tablespoon whole black peppercorns

Preheat oven to 300°F. Combine flour, ⅔ cup sugar, baking powder and black and red peppers in food processor. Melt butter in small skillet over medium heat. Cook, stirring occasionally, until browned. Add to flour mixture; process until dough forms compact ball, about 1½ minutes. Shape dough into 1-inch balls; place 1 inch apart on ungreased baking sheet. Place remaining 1 tablespoon sugar in small shallow bowl. Lightly butter bottom of flat-bottomed glass; dip glass into sugar and press each ball slightly to ½-inch thickness. Press whole peppercorn in center of each cookie. Bake on lowest rack in oven about 25 minutes or until bottoms are browned. Remove to wire rack to cool completely. Store in tightly covered container. *Makes 2 dozen*

Favorite recipe from ***American Spice Trade Association***

Chocolate Raspberry Thumbprints

1½ cups butter or margarine, softened
1 cup sugar
1 egg
1 teaspoon vanilla
3 cups all-purpose flour
¼ cup unsweetened cocoa
½ teaspoon salt
1 cup (6 ounces) semisweet mini chocolate chips
⅔ cup raspberry preserves
Powdered sugar (optional)

Preheat oven to 350°F. Grease cookie sheets. Beat butter and sugar in large bowl. Beat in egg and vanilla until light and fluffy. Mix in flour, cocoa and salt until well blended. Stir in chocolate chips. Roll level tablespoonfuls of dough into balls. Place 2 inches apart onto prepared cookie sheets. Make deep indentation in center of each ball with thumb.

Bake 12 to 15 minutes until just set. Cool 2 minutes on cookie sheets. Remove to wire racks; cool completely. Fill centers with raspberry preserves and sprinkle with powdered sugar, if desired. Store between layers of waxed paper in airtight containers.
Makes about 4½ dozen cookies

Elephant Ears

1 package (17¼ ounces) frozen puff pastry, thawed according to package directions
1 egg, beaten
¼ cup sugar, divided
2 squares (1 ounce each) semisweet chocolate

Preheat oven to 375°F. Grease cookie sheets; sprinkle lightly with water. Roll one sheet of pastry to 12×10-inch rectangle. Brush with egg; sprinkle with 1 tablespoon sugar. Tightly roll up 10-inch sides, meeting in center. Brush center with egg and seal rolls tightly together; turn over. Cut into ¼- to ½-inch-thick slices. Place slices on prepared cookie sheets. Sprinkle with 1 tablespoon sugar. Repeat with remaining pastry, egg and sugar. Bake 16 to 18 minutes until golden brown. Remove to wire racks; cool completely.

Melt chocolate in small saucepan over low heat, stirring constantly. Remove from heat. Spread bottoms of cookies with chocolate. Place on wire rack, chocolate side up. Let stand until chocolate is set. Store between layers of waxed paper in airtight containers.
Makes about 4 dozen cookies

Top to bottom: *Elephant Ears and Chocolate Raspberry Thumbprints*

SANTA'S FAVORITE BROWNIES

- 1 cup (6 ounces) milk chocolate chips
- ½ cup butter or margarine
- ¾ cup granulated sugar
- 2 eggs
- 1 teaspoon vanilla
- 1¼ cups all-purpose flour
- 3 tablespoons unsweetened cocoa
- 1 teaspoon baking powder
- ½ teaspoon salt
- ½ cup chopped walnuts
- Buttercream Frosting (recipe follows)
- Jelly beans and icing gels, for decoration (optional)

Preheat oven to 350°F. Grease 9-inch square baking pan. Melt chocolate and butter with granulated sugar in medium saucepan over low heat, stirring constantly. Pour into large bowl; add eggs and vanilla. Beat with electric mixer until well blended. Stir in flour, cocoa, baking powder and salt; blend well. Fold in walnuts. Spread into prepared pan.

Bake 25 to 30 minutes until wooden pick inserted in center comes out clean. Place pan on wire rack; cool completely. Frost with Buttercream Frosting, if desired. Cut into squares. Decorate with jelly beans and icing gels, if desired. Store in airtight container.

Makes 16 brownies

Buttercream Frosting

- 3 cups powdered sugar, sifted
- ½ cup butter or margarine, softened
- 2 to 3 tablespoons milk, divided
- ½ teaspoon vanilla

Combine powdered sugar, butter, 2 tablespoons milk and vanilla in large bowl. Beat with electric mixer at low speed until blended. Beat at high speed until light and fluffy, adding more milk, 1 teaspoon at a time, as needed for good spreading consistency.

Makes about 1½ cups frosting

SCOTTISH SHORTBREAD

- 5 cups all-purpose flour
- 1 cup rice flour
- 2 cups butter or margarine, softened
- 1 cup sugar
- Candied fruit (optional)

Preheat oven to 325°F. Sift together flours. Beat butter and sugar in large bowl with electric mixer until creamy. Blend in ¾ of flour until mixture resembles fine crumbs. Stir in remaining flour by hand. Press dough firmly into ungreased 15½×10½×1-inch jelly-roll pan *or* two 9-inch fluted tart pans; crimp and flute edges, if desired. Bake 40 to 45 minutes until light brown. Place pan on wire rack. Cut into bars or wedges while warm. Decorate with candied fruit, if desired. Cool completely. Store in airtight containers.

Makes about 4 dozen bars or 24 wedges

Santa's Favorite Brownies

MOIST PUMPKIN COOKIES

- ½ cup butter or margarine, softened
- 1 cup packed brown sugar
- ½ cup granulated sugar
- 1½ cups canned pumpkin (not pumpkin pie filling)
- 1 egg
- 1 teaspoon vanilla
- 2¼ cups all-purpose flour
- 1¼ teaspoons ground cinnamon
- 1 teaspoon baking powder
- ½ teaspoon baking soda
- ½ teaspoon salt
- ½ teaspoon ground nutmeg
- ¾ cup raisins
- ½ cup chopped walnuts
- Powdered Sugar Glaze (recipe follows)

Preheat oven to 350°F. Beat butter and sugars in large bowl until creamy. Beat in pumpkin, egg and vanilla until light and fluffy. Mix in flour, cinnamon, baking powder, baking soda, salt and nutmeg until blended. Stir in raisins and walnuts. Drop heaping tablespoonfuls of dough 2 inches apart onto ungreased cookie sheets.

Bake 12 to 15 minutes until set. Cool 2 minutes on cookie sheets. Remove to wire racks; cool completely. Drizzle Powdered Sugar Glaze onto cookies. Let glaze set. Store between layers of waxed paper in airtight containers.

Makes about 3½ dozen cookies

POWDERED SUGAR GLAZE: Combine 1 cup powdered sugar and 2 tablespoons milk in small bowl until well blended.

HOLIDAY SUGAR COOKIES

- 1 cup butter or margarine, softened
- ¾ cup sugar
- 1 egg
- 2 cups all-purpose flour
- 1 teaspoon baking powder
- ¼ teaspoon ground cinnamon
- ¼ teaspoon salt
- Colored sprinkles or sugar, for decorating (optional)

Beat butter and sugar in large bowl with electric mixer until creamy. Add egg; beat until fluffy. Stir in flour, baking powder, cinnamon and salt until well blended. Form into a ball; wrap in plastic wrap and flatten. Refrigerate about 2 hours or until firm.

Preheat oven to 350°F. Roll out dough, a small portion at a time, to ¼-inch thickness on lightly floured surface with lightly floured rolling pin. (Keep remaining dough in refrigerator.) Cut with 3-inch cookie cutter. Sprinkle with colored sprinkles, if desired. Transfer to ungreased cookie sheets.

Bake 7 to 9 minutes until edges are lightly browned. Cool 1 minute on cookie sheets. Remove to wire racks; cool completely. Store in airtight container.

Makes about 3 dozen cookies

GIFT TAG COOKIES: Prepare dough as directed; divide into 4 pieces. Shape each piece into a ball; wrap in plastic wrap. Refrigerate 2 hours or up to 3 days. Roll out each ball on lightly floured surface to ¼-inch thickness. (Keep remaining dough in refrigerator.) Cut into gift tag shapes; push drinking straw or skewer into each cookie to make ¼-inch hole. Omit colored sprinkles. Bake as directed. Spread with Buttercream Frosting (page 60) or other white icing. Pipe names and/or decorations with different colored decorators frostings and use red licorice strands as "string" for the tags.

SUGAR COOKIE GIFT BOXES: Prepare and roll out dough as directed. Cut dough into squares with pastry wheel or ravioli cutter. Bake and cool as directed. Stack 4 or 5 cookies; tie with ribbon.

CHOCOLATE-DIPPED FINGERS

- **1 cup butter or margarine, softened**
- **½ cup sifted powdered sugar**
- **1¾ cups all-purpose flour**
- **½ teaspoon almond extract**
- **3 squares (1 ounce each) semisweet chocolate, melted**
- **⅓ cup ground almonds**

Preheat oven to 350°F. Grease cookie sheets. Beat butter and powdered sugar in large bowl until creamy. Mix in flour and almond extract until well blended. Place ½-inch round or star tip in pastry bag; add dough. Pipe 2½-inch lengths of dough onto prepared cookie sheets.

Bake 13 to 16 minutes until set. Cool 1 minute on cookie sheets. Remove to wire racks; cool completely. Dip one cookie end into chocolate; shake off excess. Sprinkle chocolate end with almonds. Repeat with remaining cookies. Let chocolate set. Store in airtight containers.

Makes about 4½ dozen cookies

OAT-Y NUT BARS

- **½ cup butter or margarine**
- **½ cup honey**
- **¼ cup corn syrup**
- **¼ cup packed brown sugar**
- **2¾ cups uncooked quick oats**
- **⅔ cup raisins**
- **½ cup salted peanuts**

Preheat oven to 300°F. Grease 9-inch square baking pan. Melt butter with honey, corn syrup and brown sugar in medium saucepan over medium heat, stirring constantly. Bring to a boil; boil 8 minutes or until mixture thickens slightly. Stir in oats, raisins and peanuts until well blended. Press evenly into prepared pan.

Bake 45 to 50 minutes until golden brown. Place pan on wire rack; score top into squares. Cool completely. Cut into bars.

Makes 16 bars

HOMEMADE COCONUT MACAROONS

- **3 egg whites**
- **¼ teaspoon cream of tartar**
- **⅛ teaspoon salt**
- **¾ cup sugar**
- **2¼ cups shredded coconut, toasted***
- **1 teaspoon vanilla**

*To toast coconut, spread evenly on cookie sheet. Toast in 350°F oven for 3 minutes. Stir and toast 1 to 2 minutes more until light golden brown.

Preheat oven to 325°F. Line cookie sheets with parchment paper or foil. Beat egg whites, cream of tartar and salt in large bowl with electric mixer until soft peaks form. Beat in sugar, 1 tablespoon at a time, until egg whites are stiff and shiny. Fold in coconut and vanilla. Drop tablespoonfuls of dough 4 inches apart onto prepared cookie sheets; spread each into 3-inch circles with back of spoon.

Bake 18 to 22 minutes until light brown. Cool 1 minute on cookie sheets. Remove to wire racks; cool completely. Store in airtight container.

Makes about 2 dozen cookies

HONEY SPICE BALLS

- **½ cup butter or margarine, softened**
- **½ cup packed brown sugar**
- **1 egg**
- **1 tablespoon honey**
- **1 teaspoon vanilla**
- **2 cups all-purpose flour**
- **½ teaspoon baking powder**
- **½ teaspoon ground cinnamon**
- **¼ teaspoon ground nutmeg**
- **Uncooked quick oats**

Preheat oven to 350°F. Grease cookie sheets. Beat butter and brown sugar in large bowl with electric mixer until creamy. Add egg, honey and vanilla; beat until light and fluffy. Stir in flour, baking powder, cinnamon and nutmeg until well blended. Shape tablespoonfuls of dough into balls; roll in oats. Place 2 inches apart on prepared cookie sheets.

Bake 15 to 18 minutes until cookie tops crack slightly. Cool 1 minute on cookie sheets. Remove to wire racks; cool completely. Store in airtight container.

Makes about 2½ dozen cookies

Left to right: *Homemade Coconut Macaroons and Honey Spice Balls*

SANTA'S STOCKINGS

½ cup (1 stick) margarine or butter, softened
⅔ cup firmly packed brown sugar
¼ cup granulated sugar
1 egg
2 tablespoons milk
1 teaspoon almond extract
¾ cup all-purpose flour
½ teaspoon baking soda
¼ teaspoon salt (optional)
2½ cups QUAKER® Oats (quick or old fashioned, uncooked)
1 cup dried cherries or dried cranberries
1 cup coarsely chopped almonds (optional)
Decorator's icing
Assorted small candies

Preheat oven to 350°F.* Lightly grease two cookie sheets. Beat together margarine and sugars until creamy. Add egg, milk and almond extract; beat well. Add combined flour, baking soda and salt; mix well. Stir in oats, dried cherries and almonds; mix well. Divide dough into 4 equal portions. With moistened hands, pat dough onto prepared cookie sheets into ¼-inch-thick holiday shapes such as stockings, Christmas trees or candy canes. Bake 12 to 14 minutes or until edges are light golden brown. Cool 2 minutes on cookie sheets; carefully remove to wire racks. Cool completely. Decorate as desired. Store in tightly covered container. *Makes 4 jumbo cookies*

*For drop cookies, preheat oven to 375°F. Follow recipe as directed except drop dough by rounded tablespoonfuls onto ungreased cookie sheet. Bake 10 to 12 minutes or until light golden brown. Cool 1 minute on cookie sheet; remove to wire rack. Cool completely. *Makes about 3 dozen cookies*

ORANGE-CASHEW COOKIES

½ cup butter or margarine, softened
⅔ cup sugar
1 egg
1 teaspoon grated orange peel
3 tablespoons orange juice
2 cups all-purpose flour
1 teaspoon baking soda
¼ teaspoon salt
1 cup chopped cashews

Preheat oven to 350°F. Beat butter and sugar in large bowl until creamy. Beat in egg, orange peel and juice until light and fluffy. Mix in flour, baking soda and salt until well blended. Stir in cashews. Drop tablespoonfuls of dough 2 inches apart onto ungreased cookie sheets.

Bake 9 minutes or until lightly browned. Remove to wire racks; cool completely. Store in airtight container. *Makes about 1½ dozen cookies*

Santa's Stocking

SANTA

GINGERBREAD PEOPLE

½ cup butter or margarine, softened
½ cup packed brown sugar
⅓ cup molasses
⅓ cup water
1 egg
4 cups all-purpose flour
2 teaspoons baking soda
1 teaspoon ground ginger
½ teaspoon ground allspice
½ teaspoon ground cinnamon
½ teaspoon ground cloves
White or colored decorators frostings

Beat butter and brown sugar in large bowl with electric mixer until creamy. Add molasses, water and egg; beat until blended. Stir in flour, baking soda, ginger, allspice, cinnamon and cloves until well blended. Cover; refrigerate about 2 hours or until firm.

Preheat oven to 350°F. Grease cookie sheets. Roll out dough to ⅛-inch thickness on lightly floured surface with lightly floured rolling pin. Cut with cookie cutter. Place 2 inches apart on prepared cookie sheets.

Bake 12 to 15 minutes until firm to the touch. Cool 1 minute on cookie sheets. Remove to wire racks; cool completely. Decorate with frostings. Store in airtight containers.

Makes about 4½ dozen cookies

OLD WORLD PFEFFERNÜSSE COOKIES

½ cup butter or margarine, softened
¾ cup packed brown sugar
½ cup molasses
1 egg
1 tablespoon licorice-flavored liqueur (optional)
3¼ cups all-purpose flour
1 teaspoon baking soda
1 teaspoon ground cinnamon
½ teaspoon ground cloves
¼ teaspoon ground nutmeg
Dash pepper
Powdered sugar

Preheat oven to 350°F. Grease cookie sheets. Beat butter and brown sugar in large bowl until creamy. Beat in molasses, egg and liqueur, if desired, until light and fluffy. Mix in flour, baking soda, cinnamon, cloves, nutmeg and pepper. Shape level tablespoonfuls of dough into balls. Place 2 inches apart onto prepared cookie sheets.

Bake 12 to 14 minutes until set. Cool 2 minutes on cookie sheets. Remove to wire racks; sprinkle with powdered sugar. Cool completely. Store in airtight containers. *Makes about 4 dozen cookies*

Left to right: *Holiday Sugar Cookies (page 62) and Gingerbread People*

GOOEY CARAMEL CHOCOLATE BARS

2 cups all-purpose flour
1 cup granulated sugar
¼ teaspoon salt
2 cups butter or margarine, divided
1 cup packed light brown sugar
⅓ cup light corn syrup
1 cup semisweet chocolate chips

Preheat oven to 350°F. Line 13×9-inch baking pan with foil. Combine flour, granulated sugar and salt in medium bowl; stir until blended. Cut in 14 tablespoons (1¾ sticks) butter until mixture resembles coarse crumbs. Press into bottom of prepared pan. Bake 18 to 20 minutes until lightly browned around edges. Remove pan to wire rack; cool completely.

Combine 1 cup butter, brown sugar and corn syrup in heavy medium saucepan. Cook over medium heat 5 to 8 minutes until mixture boils, stirring frequently. Boil gently 2 minutes, without stirring. Immediately pour over cooled base; spread evenly to edges. Cool completely.

Melt chocolate in double boiler over hot (not simmering) water. Stir in remaining 2 tablespoons butter. Pour over cooled caramel layer and spread evenly to edges of pan with metal spatula. Refrigerate 10 to 15 minutes until chocolate begins to set. Remove; cool completely. Cut into bars.

Makes 3 dozen bars

ALMOND CRESCENTS

1 cup butter or margarine, softened
⅓ cup granulated sugar
1¾ cups all-purpose flour
¼ cup cornstarch
1 teaspoon vanilla
1½ cups ground almonds, toasted*
Chocolate Glaze (recipe follows) *or* powdered sugar

*To toast almonds, spread on cookie sheet. Bake at 325°F for 4 minutes or until fragrant and golden.

Preheat oven to 325°F. Beat butter and granulated sugar in large bowl until creamy. Mix in flour, cornstarch and vanilla. Stir in almonds. Shape tablespoonfuls of dough into crescents. Place 2 inches apart on ungreased cookie sheets. Bake 22 to 25 minutes until light brown. Cool 1 minute. Remove to wire racks; cool completely. Drizzle with Chocolate Glaze, if desired. Allow chocolate to set, then store in airtight container. Or, before serving, sprinkle with powdered sugar.

Makes about 3 dozen cookies

CHOCOLATE GLAZE: Place ½ cup semisweet chocolate chips and 1 tablespoon butter or margarine in small resealable plastic bag. Place bag in bowl of hot water for 2 to 3 minutes until chocolate is softened. Dry with paper towel. Knead until chocolate is smooth. Snip pinpoint corner in bag. Drizzle chocolate over cookies.

SPICED DATE BARS

½ cup margarine, softened
1 cup packed brown sugar
2 eggs
¾ cup light sour cream
2 cups all-purpose flour
1 teaspoon baking soda
1 teaspoon ground cinnamon
½ teaspoon ground nutmeg
1 package (8 or 10 ounces) DOLE® Chopped Dates or Pitted Dates, chopped
Powdered sugar (optional)

• Beat margarine and brown sugar until light and fluffy. Beat in eggs, one at a time. Stir in sour cream.

• Combine dry ingredients. Beat into sour cream mixture. Stir in dates. Spread batter evenly into greased 13×9-inch baking pan.

• Bake at 350°F 25 to 30 minutes or until toothpick inserted in center comes out clean. Cool completely in pan on wire rack.

• Cut into bars. Dust with powdered sugar.

Makes 24 bars

Prep Time: 15 minutes
Bake Time: 30 minutes

LOADED OATMEAL COOKIES

¾ cup butter or margarine, softened
1 cup packed brown sugar
1 egg
1 tablespoon milk
1 teaspoon vanilla
1½ cups uncooked quick oats
1 cup all-purpose flour
½ teaspoon baking soda
½ teaspoon salt
½ teaspoon ground cinnamon
1 cup (6 ounces) semisweet chocolate chips
1 cup (6 ounces) butterscotch chips
¾ cup raisins
½ cup chopped walnuts

Preheat oven to 350°F. Beat butter and brown sugar in large bowl until creamy. Beat in egg, milk and vanilla until light and fluffy. Mix in oats, flour, baking soda, salt and cinnamon until well blended. Stir in chips, raisins and walnuts. Drop rounded tablespoonfuls of dough 2 inches apart onto ungreased cookie sheets.

Bake 12 to 15 minutes until lightly browned around edges. Cool 2 minutes on cookie sheets. Remove to wire racks; cool completely. Store in airtight container. *Makes about 3 dozen cookies*

OAT PECAN PRALINES

- 1 cup (2 sticks) margarine or butter, softened
- 1¼ cups firmly packed brown sugar
- 2 eggs
- 2 tablespoons molasses
- 1 teaspoon maple flavoring
- 1¼ cups all-purpose flour
- 1 teaspoon baking soda
- 2½ cups QUAKER® Oats (quick or old fashioned, uncooked)
- 1 cup pecans, coarsely chopped
- ¾ cup pecan halves (about 48 halves)

Beat together margarine and sugar until creamy. Add eggs, molasses and maple flavoring; beat well. Add combined flour and baking soda; mix well. Stir in oats and chopped nuts; mix well. Cover dough; chill at least 1 hour.

Preheat oven to 350°F. Lightly grease cookie sheet. Shape dough into 1-inch balls. Place 3 inches apart on prepared cookie sheet. Flatten each ball by pressing a pecan half in center. Bake 10 to 12 minutes or until deep golden brown. Immediately remove to wire rack; cool completely. Store in tightly covered container.

Makes about 4 dozen cookies

CINNAMONY APPLE STREUSEL BARS

- 1¼ cups graham cracker crumbs
- 1¼ cups all-purpose flour
- ¾ cup packed brown sugar, divided
- ¼ cup granulated sugar
- 1 teaspoon ground cinnamon
- ¾ cup butter or margarine, melted
- 2 cups chopped apples (2 medium apples, cored and peeled)
- Glaze (recipe follows)

Preheat oven to 350°F. Grease 13×9-inch baking pan. Combine graham cracker crumbs, flour, ½ cup brown sugar, granulated sugar, cinnamon and butter in large bowl until well blended; reserve 1 cup. Press remaining crumb mixture into bottom of prepared pan.

Bake 8 minutes. Remove from oven; set aside. Toss apples with remaining ¼ cup brown sugar in medium bowl until brown sugar is dissolved; arrange apples over baked crust. Sprinkle reserved 1 cup crumb mixture over filling. Bake 30 to 35 minutes more until apples are tender. Remove pan to wire rack; cool completely. Drizzle with Glaze. Cut into bars.

Makes 3 dozen bars

GLAZE: Combine ½ cup powdered sugar and 1 tablespoon milk in small bowl until well blended.

Oat Pecan Pralines

LEMONY BUTTER COOKIES

½ cup butter, softened
½ cup sugar
1 egg
1½ cups all-purpose flour
2 tablespoons fresh lemon juice
1 teaspoon grated lemon peel
½ teaspoon baking powder
⅛ teaspoon salt
Additional sugar

Beat butter and sugar in large bowl with electric mixer until creamy. Beat in egg until light and fluffy. Mix in flour, lemon juice and peel, baking powder and salt. Cover; refrigerate about 2 hours or until firm.

Preheat oven to 350°F. Roll out dough, a small portion at a time, to ¼-inch thickness on well-floured surface with floured rolling pin. (Keep remaining dough in refrigerator.) Cut with 3-inch round cookie cutter. Transfer to ungreased cookie sheets. Sprinkle with sugar.

Bake 8 to 10 minutes until lightly browned on edges. Cool 1 minute on cookie sheets. Remove to wire racks; cool completely. Store in airtight container. *Makes about 2½ dozen cookies*

FESTIVE LEBKUCHEN

3 tablespoons butter or margarine
1 cup packed brown sugar
¼ cup honey
1 egg
Grated peel and juice of 1 lemon
3 cups all-purpose flour
2 teaspoons ground allspice
½ teaspoon baking soda
½ teaspoon salt
White decorators frosting

Melt butter with brown sugar and honey in medium saucepan over low heat, stirring constantly. Pour into large bowl. Cool 30 minutes. Add egg, lemon peel and juice; beat 2 minutes with electric mixer at high speed. Stir in flour, allspice, baking soda and salt until well blended. Cover; refrigerate overnight or up to 3 days.

Preheat oven to 350°F. Grease cookie sheet. Roll out dough to ½-inch thickness on lightly floured surface with lightly floured rolling pin. Cut with 3-inch cookie cutter. Transfer to prepared cookie sheet. Bake 15 to 18 minutes until edges are light brown. Cool 1 minute. Remove to wire rack; cool completely. Decorate with white frosting. Store in airtight container. *Makes 1 dozen cookies*

Lemony Butter Cookies

CHOC-OAT-CHIP COOKIES

1 cup (2 sticks) margarine or butter, softened
1¼ cups firmly packed brown sugar
½ cup granulated sugar
2 eggs
2 tablespoons milk
2 teaspoons vanilla
1¾ cups all-purpose flour
1 teaspoon baking soda
½ teaspoon salt (optional)
2½ cups QUAKER® Oats (quick or old fashioned, uncooked)
1 (12-ounce) package (2 cups) semisweet chocolate morsels
1 cup coarsely chopped nuts (optional)

Preheat oven to 375°F. Beat together margarine and sugars until creamy. Add eggs, milk and vanilla; beat well. Add combined flour, baking soda and salt; mix well. Stir in oats, chocolate morsels and nuts; mix well. Drop by rounded tablespoonfuls onto ungreased cookie sheet.* Bake 9 to 10 minutes for a chewy cookie or 12 to 13 minutes for a crisp cookie. Cool 1 minute on cookie sheet; remove to wire rack. Cool completely. Store in tightly covered container.

Makes about 5 dozen

*FOR BAR COOKIES: Press dough onto bottom of ungreased 13×9-inch baking pan. Bake 35 to 40 minutes or until light golden brown. Cool completely; cut into bars. Store tightly covered.

Makes about 3 dozen

VARIATIONS:
RAISIN SPICE OATMEAL COOKIES: Prepare cookies as recipe directs, adding 1 teaspoon ground cinnamon and ¼ teaspoon ground nutmeg to dry ingredients. Substitute 1 cup raisins for chocolate morsels.

SIGNATURE OATMEAL COOKIES: Prepare cookies as recipe directs except substitute 1 cup (any combination of) raisins, diced dried mixed fruit, crushed toffee pieces or candy coated chocolate pieces for 1 cup chocolate morsels.

Choc-Oat-Chip Cookies

CHOCOLATE CHIP CRANBERRY CHEESE BARS

- 1 cup (2 sticks) butter or margarine, softened
- 1 cup packed brown sugar
- 2 cups all-purpose flour
- 1½ cups quick or old-fashioned oats, uncooked
- 2 teaspoons grated orange peel
- 2 cups (12-ounce package) NESTLÉ® TOLL HOUSE® Semi-Sweet Chocolate Morsels
- 1 cup (4 ounces) dried cranberries
- 1 package (8 ounces) cream cheese, softened
- 1¼ cups (14-ounce can) CARNATION® Sweetened Condensed Milk

BEAT butter and brown sugar in large mixer bowl until creamy; beat in flour, oats and orange peel until crumbly. Stir in morsels and cranberries; reserve 2 cups mixture. Press remaining mixture onto bottom of greased 13×9-inch baking pan.

BAKE in preheated 350°F oven for 15 minutes. Beat cream cheese in small mixer bowl until smooth. Gradually beat in sweetened condensed milk. Pour over hot crust; sprinkle with reserved oat mixture.

BAKE at 350°F for 25 to 30 minutes or until center is set. Cool in pan on wire rack.

Makes about 3 dozen bars

FRUITCAKE COOKIES

- ½ cup butter or margarine, softened
- ¾ cup sugar
- ½ cup milk
- 1 egg
- 2 tablespoons orange juice
- 1 tablespoon vinegar
- 2 cups all-purpose flour
- 1 teaspoon baking powder
- ½ teaspoon baking soda
- ¼ teaspoon salt
- ½ cup chopped walnuts
- ½ cup chopped candied mixed fruit
- ½ cup raisins
- ¼ cup chopped dried pineapple
- Powdered sugar

Preheat oven to 350°F. Grease cookie sheets. Beat butter and sugar in large bowl until creamy. Beat in milk, egg, orange juice and vinegar until blended. Mix in flour, baking powder, baking soda and salt. Stir in walnuts, mixed fruit, raisins and pineapple. Drop rounded tablespoonfuls of dough 2 inches apart onto prepared cookie sheets.

Bake 12 to 14 minutes until lightly browned around edges. Cool 2 minutes on cookie sheets. Remove to wire racks; cool completely. Dust with powdered sugar. Store in airtight container.

Makes about 2½ dozen cookies

ABSOLUTELY WONDERFUL PECAN BARS

1½ cups quick or old-fashioned oats
1½ cups all-purpose flour
1 cup JACK FROST® dark brown sugar
1½ cups butter, divided
1½ cups *or* 1 (7-ounce) package pecan halves
1 cup JACK FROST® dark brown sugar, packed
1 cup JACK FROST® granulated sugar
⅓ cup heavy cream
2 teaspoons vanilla

In large bowl, combine oats, flour and 1 cup dark brown sugar. Cut ½ cup butter into mixture until coarse and crumbly. Press into 13×9-inch baking pan. Place pecans evenly over crumb mixture.

In heavy saucepan, combine remaining 1 cup dark brown sugar, granulated sugar and remaining 1 cup butter. Bring to a full rolling boil over medium heat, stirring constantly. Boil 3 minutes; remove from heat. Stir in heavy cream and vanilla until well blended; pour over pecans. Bake in 350°F oven 35 to 40 minutes. Cool in pan; cut into bars.

Makes 48 bars

YULETIDE LINZER BARS

1⅓ cups butter or margarine, softened
¾ cup sugar
1 egg
1 teaspoon lemon peel
2½ cups all-purpose flour
1½ cups whole almonds, ground
1 teaspoon ground cinnamon
¾ cup raspberry preserves
Powdered sugar

Preheat oven to 350°F. Grease 13×9-inch baking pan. Beat butter and sugar in large bowl until creamy. Beat in egg and lemon peel until blended. Mix in flour, almonds and cinnamon until well blended. Press 2 cups flour mixture into bottom of prepared pan. Spread preserves over crust. Press remaining flour mixture, a small amount at a time, evenly over preserves. Bake 35 to 40 minutes until golden brown. Remove pan to wire rack; cool completely. Sprinkle with powdered sugar. Cut into bars.

Makes 3 dozen bars

HOLIDAY CANDIES

MERRI-MINT TRUFFLES

1 package (10 ounces) mint chocolate chips
1/3 cup whipping cream
1/4 cup butter or margarine
1 container (3 1/2 ounces) chocolate sprinkles

Melt chocolate chips with cream and butter in heavy medium saucepan over low heat, stirring occasionally. Pour into pie pan. Refrigerate about 2 hours or until mixture is fudgy, but soft.

Shape about 1 tablespoonful of mixture into 1 1/4-inch ball. Repeat with remaining mixture. Roll balls in your palms to form uniform round shapes; place on waxed paper.

Place sprinkles in shallow bowl. Roll balls in sprinkles; place in petit four or candy cases. (If coating mixture won't stick because truffle has set, roll between your palms until outside is soft.) Store in airtight container up to 3 days in refrigerator or several weeks in freezer.

Makes about 24 truffles

Top box (left to right): Merri-Mint Truffles, Easy Orange Truffles (page 88) and Jolly Bourbon Balls (page 99)

CANDIED ORANGE AND GRAPEFRUIT PEELS

2 large pink grapefruits
3 large oranges
3½ cups granulated sugar, divided

Divide peel of each grapefruit and orange into 4 segments by inserting sharp knife and cutting only as deep as the peel. Carefully remove peel (including white pith) in 4 pieces. Save fruit for another use. Cut each quarter into 8 to 9 lengthwise strips.

Place peels and enough water to cover in large saucepan. Bring to a boil. Cook over medium heat 8 to 10 minutes; drain. Repeat step two more times to remove bitterness of peels. Set aside.

Add 3 cups sugar to 2¼ cups water in large saucepan. Bring to a boil, stirring to dissolve sugar. Add strips of peel and simmer over low heat, stirring occasionally, until nearly all syrup is absorbed, about 45 minutes.

With tongs, transfer peels to wire rack or sheet of waxed paper sprayed with nonstick cooking spray. Let cool at least 3 hours.

Place remaining ½ cup sugar in paper bag. Add peels and gently toss, shaking off excess.

The peels can be stored in an airtight container, with waxed paper between each layer, in cool place up to 3 months.

Makes about 70 grapefruit slices and 90 orange slices

NOTE: To make only grapefruit or orange peels, double the number of grapefruits or oranges.

Favorite recipe from ***The Sugar Association, Inc.***

SPICE 'N SUGAR POPCORN

1 cup sugar
1 teaspoon LAWRY'S® Seasoned Salt
1 teaspoon ground cinnamon
½ teaspoon ground nutmeg
½ teaspoon ground cloves
½ cup water
½ cup walnut halves
1 quart popped popcorn

In medium saucepan, combine sugar, Seasoned Salt and spices; add water and blend well until sugar dissolves. Bring to a boil; reduce heat and simmer, uncovered, 5 to 7 minutes to soft-ball stage (236°F). Remove from heat and add walnut halves. In large bowl, combine popcorn with syrup mixture; toss to coat. Turn out onto waxed paper and cool. Store in an airtight container.

Makes about 1 quart

Candied Orange and Grapefruit Peels

DOUBLE DIPPED APPLES

- MAZOLA No Stick® corn oil cooking spray
- 5 medium apples
- 5 wooden sticks
- 1 package (14 ounces) caramel candies, unwrapped
- ¼ cup KARO® Light or Dark Corn Syrup
- ¾ cup chopped walnuts
- 1 cup (6 ounces) semisweet chocolate chips
- 1 teaspoon MAZOLA® corn oil

Spray small cookie sheet with cooking spray; set aside. Wash and dry apples; insert stick into stem end.

In small, deep microwavable bowl, microwave caramels and corn syrup on HIGH (100%) 3 to 4 minutes or until caramels are melted and smooth, stirring after each minute. Dip apples in hot caramel mixture, turning to coat well. Allow caramel to drip from apples for a few seconds, then scrape excess from bottom of apples. Roll bottom half in walnuts. Place on prepared cookie sheet. Refrigerate at least 15 minutes.

In small microwavable bowl, microwave chocolate and corn oil on HIGH 1 to 2 minutes; stir until melted. Drizzle apples with chocolate. Refrigerate 10 minutes or until chocolate is firm. Wrap apples individually; store in refrigerator.

Makes 5 apples

Prep Time: 20 minutes, plus cooling

CREAMY CARAMELS

- ½ cup slivered or chopped toasted almonds (optional)
- 1 cup butter or margarine, cut into small pieces
- 1 can (14 ounces) sweetened condensed milk
- 2 cups sugar
- 1 cup light corn syrup
- 1½ teaspoons vanilla

Line 8-inch square baking pan with foil, extending edges over sides of pan. Lightly grease foil; sprinkle almonds over bottom of pan, if desired.

Melt butter in heavy 2-quart saucepan over low heat. Add milk, sugar and corn syrup. Stir over low heat until sugar is dissolved and mixture comes to a boil. Carefully clip candy thermometer to side of pan (do not let bulb touch bottom of pan). Cook over low heat about 30 minutes or until thermometer registers 240°F (soft-ball stage), stirring occasionally. Immediately remove from heat and stir in vanilla. Pour mixture into prepared pan. Cool completely.

Lift caramels out of pan using foil; remove foil. Place on cutting board; cut into 1-inch squares with sharp knife. Wrap each square in plastic wrap. Store in airtight container.

Makes about 2½ pounds or 64 caramels

Double Dipped Apples

CHOCOLATE MINT SQUARES

6 tablespoons butter (do not use margarine)
½ cup HERSHEY®'S Cocoa
2 cups powdered sugar
3 tablespoons plus 1 teaspoon milk, divided
1 teaspoon vanilla extract
Mint Filling (recipe follows)

Line 8-inch square pan with foil, extending foil over edges of pan. In small saucepan over low heat, melt butter; add cocoa. Cook, stirring constantly, just until mixture is smooth. Remove from heat; add powdered sugar, 3 tablespoons milk and vanilla. Cook over low heat, stirring constantly, until mixture is glossy. Spread half of mixture into prepared pan. Refrigerate. Meanwhile, prepare Mint Filling; spread filling over chocolate layer. Refrigerate 10 minutes. To remaining chocolate mixture in saucepan, add remaining 1 teaspoon milk. Cook over low heat, stirring constantly, until smooth. Spread quickly over filling. Refrigerate until firm. Use foil to lift candy out of pan; peel off foil. Cut candy into squares. Store in tightly covered container in refrigerator.

Makes about 4 dozen pieces

Mint Filling

1 package (3 ounces) cream cheese, softened
2 cups powdered sugar
½ teaspoon vanilla extract
¼ teaspoon peppermint extract
3 to 5 drops green food color

In small mixer bowl, beat cream cheese, powdered sugar, vanilla, peppermint extract and food color until smooth. Add 2 to 3 teaspoons milk, if needed, for spreading consistency.

WILD PEANUT BUTTER BALLS

1 cup well-cooked wild rice, chopped
½ cup chopped walnuts or pecans
¼ cup chopped dates
¼ cup chopped raisins
½ cup peanut butter
2 tablespoons molasses
2 tablespoons orange juice
½ cup flaked coconut

Combine wild rice, walnuts, dates and raisins in medium bowl. Stir in peanut butter, molasses and orange juice until well combined. Roll mixture into ½-inch balls; roll each ball in coconut. Refrigerate in airtight container at least 3 hours to allow flavors to blend. Serve within 1 to 2 days.

Makes about 25 balls

Favorite recipe from ***Minnesota Cultivated Wild Rice Council***

Left to right: *Chocolate Chip Peanut Butter Fudge (page 98), Hershey®'s Vanilla Milk Chips Almond Fudge (page 94) and Chocolate Mint Squares*

EASY ORANGE TRUFFLES

1 cup (6 ounces) semisweet chocolate chips
2 squares (1 ounce each) unsweetened chocolate, chopped
1½ cups powdered sugar
½ cup butter or margarine, softened
1 tablespoon grated orange peel
1 tablespoon orange-flavored liqueur
2 squares (1 ounce each) semisweet chocolate, grated or cocoa

Melt chocolate chips and unsweetened chocolate in heavy small saucepan over very low heat, stirring constantly; set aside.

Combine powdered sugar, butter, orange peel and liqueur in small bowl. Beat with electric mixer until combined. Beat in cooled chocolate. Pour into pie pan. Refrigerate about 30 minutes or until mixture is fudgy and can be shaped into balls.

Shape scant 1 tablespoonful of mixture into 1-inch ball. Repeat with remaining mixture. Roll balls in your palms to form uniform round shapes; place on waxed paper.

Sprinkle grated chocolate or cocoa in shallow bowl. Roll balls in grated chocolate or cocoa; place in petit four or candy cases. (If coating mixture won't stick because truffle has set, roll between your palms until outside is soft.) Store in airtight container up to 3 days in refrigerator or several weeks in freezer.

Makes about 34 truffles

TIP: Truffles are coated with cocoa, powdered sugar, nuts, sprinkles or cookie crumbs to add flavor and prevent the truffle from melting in your fingers.

MAPLE WALNUT FUDGE

2 tablespoons butter or margarine
⅔ cup *undiluted* CARNATION® Evaporated Milk
1½ cups granulated sugar
¼ teaspoon salt
2 cups (4 ounces) mini marshmallows
2 cups (12-ounce package) NESTLÉ® TOLL HOUSE® Premier White Morsels
½ cup chopped walnuts
1½ teaspoons maple flavoring
About 50 walnut halves or pieces

COMBINE butter, evaporated milk, sugar and salt in medium, heavy saucepan. Bring to a boil over medium heat, stirring constantly. Boil for 4½ to 5 minutes, stirring constantly. Remove from heat.

STIR in marshmallows, morsels, nuts and maple flavoring. Stir vigorously for 1 minute or until marshmallows are melted. Pour into foil-lined 13×9-inch baking pan. Place walnut halves in rows, spacing about ½ inch apart on top of fudge. Press into fudge. Chill until firm. Cut into squares with 1 walnut half per square.

Makes about 50 pieces

CHOCOLATE-DIPPED PEANUT BUTTER CANDIES

Dipping Chocolate (recipe follows)
½ cup creamy peanut butter
6 tablespoons butter or margarine, softened
1 tablespoon light corn syrup
1 teaspoon vanilla
2 cups powdered sugar
1 cup graham cracker crumbs

Line large cookie sheet with waxed paper. Prepare Dipping Chocolate; keep warm. Beat peanut butter, butter, corn syrup and vanilla in large bowl with electric mixer at medium speed until smooth, scraping down side of bowl once. Beat in powdered sugar and graham cracker crumbs on low speed until well mixed, scraping down side of bowl once. (Mixture will look dry.) Shape level tablespoonfuls of peanut butter mixture into balls. Place on prepared cookie sheet. Dip one ball into Dipping Chocolate. Lift coated ball out of chocolate with fork, tapping fork on side of cup to remove excess chocolate. Place on prepared cookie sheet. Repeat with remaining balls. Let chocolate set completely before storing in airtight container.

Makes about 2½ dozen candies

DIPPING CHOCOLATE: Place 1 cup (6 ounces) semisweet chocolate chips and 2 tablespoons vegetable shortening in 1-cup glass measuring cup. Microwave on HIGH (100%) about 2 minutes or until melted, stirring after 1½ minutes.

CANDIED LEMON PEELS

6 large lemons
1½ cups sugar, divided

Divide peel of each lemon into 4 segments by inserting sharp knife and cutting only as deep as the peel. Carefully remove peel (including white pith) in 4 pieces. Save fruit for another use. Cut each quarter into 4 lengthwise strips.

Place peels and enough water to cover in large saucepan. Bring to a boil. Cook over medium heat 8 to 10 minutes; drain. Repeat step two more times to remove bitterness of peel. Set aside.

Add 1 cup sugar to ¾ cup water in large saucepan. Bring to a boil, stirring to dissolve sugar. Add strips of peel and simmer over low heat, stirring occasionally, until nearly all syrup is absorbed, about 45 minutes.

With tongs, transfer peels to wire rack or sheet of waxed paper sprayed with nonstick cooking spray. Let cool at least 3 hours.

Place remaining ½ cup sugar in paper bag. Add peels and gently toss, shaking off excess.

The peels can be stored in an airtight container, with waxed paper between each layer, in cool place up to 3 months. *Makes about 96 lemon slices*

Favorite recipe from **The Sugar Association, Inc.**

Elegant Cream Cheese Mints

- **Chocolate Topping (recipe follows), optional**
- **1 package (3 ounces) cream cheese, softened**
- **3 tablespoons butter or margarine, softened**
- **½ teaspoon vanilla**
- **¼ to ½ teaspoon desired food coloring**
- **¼ teaspoon peppermint extract**
- **1 pound powdered sugar (3½ to 4 cups)**
- **⅓ cup granulated sugar**

Line large cookie sheet with waxed paper. Prepare Chocolate Topping, if desired; keep warm.

Beat cream cheese, butter, vanilla, food coloring and peppermint extract in large bowl with electric mixer at medium speed until smooth. Gradually beat in powdered sugar on low speed until well combined, scraping side of bowl several times. (If necessary stir in remaining powdered sugar with wooden spoon.)

Place granulated sugar in shallow bowl. Roll 2 teaspoons of cream cheese mixture into a ball. Roll ball in granulated sugar until coated. Flatten ball with fingers or fork to make a patty. Place patty on prepared cookie sheet. Repeat with remaining cream cheese mixture and sugar. Drizzle patties with topping, if desired. Refrigerate until firm. Store in airtight container in refrigerator.

Makes about 1½ pounds or 40 (1-inch) mints

CHOCOLATE TOPPING: Place ½ cup semisweet chocolate chips and 1 tablespoon vegetable shortening in 1-cup glass measuring cup. Microwave on HIGH (100%) about 2 minutes or until melted, stirring after 1½ minutes.

Citrus Candied Nuts

- **1 egg white**
- **1½ cups whole almonds**
- **1½ cups pecan halves**
- **1 cup powdered sugar**
- **2 tablespoons lemon juice**
- **2 teaspoons grated orange peel**
- **1 teaspoon grated lemon peel**
- **⅛ teaspoon ground nutmeg**

Preheat oven to 300°F. Generously grease 15½×10½×1-inch jelly-roll pan. Beat egg white in medium bowl with electric mixer at high speed until soft peaks form. Add almonds and pecans; stir until coated. Stir in powdered sugar, lemon juice, orange peel, lemon peel and nutmeg. Turn out onto prepared pan, spreading nuts in single layer.

Bake 30 minutes, stirring after 20 minutes. *Turn off oven.* Let nuts stand in oven 15 minutes more. Immediately remove nuts from pan to sheet of foil. Cool completely. Store up to 2 weeks in airtight container.

Makes about 3 cups nuts

Top to bottom: *Citrus Candied Nuts and Elegant Cream Cheese Mints*

TRADITIONAL PEANUT BRITTLE

- 1½ cups salted peanuts
- 1 cup sugar
- 1 cup light corn syrup
- ¼ cup water
- 2 tablespoons butter or margarine
- ¼ teaspoon baking soda

Heavily butter large cookie sheet. Place peanuts in ungreased 8-inch square baking pan. To warm peanuts, place in oven and heat oven to 250°F.

Meanwhile, place sugar, corn syrup, water and butter in heavy 2-quart saucepan. Stir over medium-low heat until sugar has dissolved and mixture comes to a boil, being careful not to splash sugar mixture on side of pan. Carefully clip candy thermometer to side of pan (do not let bulb touch bottom of pan). Cook over medium-low heat until thermometer registers 280°F, without stirring. Gradually stir in warm peanuts. Cook until thermometer registers 300°F, stirring frequently.

Immediately remove from heat; stir in baking soda until thoroughly blended. (Mixture will froth and foam.) Immediately pour onto prepared cookie sheet. Spread mixture evenly to form an even layer. Cool about 30 minutes or until set. Break brittle into pieces. Store in airtight container.

Makes about 1½ pounds

DARK CHOCOLATE FUDGE

- ½ cup whipping cream
- ½ cup light corn syrup
- 3 cups (18 ounces) semisweet chocolate chips
- 1½ cups powdered sugar, sifted
- ½ cup chopped walnuts (optional)
- 1½ teaspoons vanilla

Line 8-inch square baking pan with foil, extending edges over sides of pan.

Bring cream and corn syrup to a boil in heavy 2-quart saucepan over medium heat. Boil 1 minute. Reduce heat to low. Stir in chocolate. Cook until chocolate is melted, stirring constantly. Stir in powdered sugar, walnuts and vanilla. Pour into prepared pan. Spread mixture into corners. Cover; refrigerate 2 hours or until firm.

Lift fudge out of pan using foil; remove foil. Place on cutting board; cut into 1-inch squares. Store in airtight container.

Makes about 2 pounds or 64 candies

PEANUT BUTTER FUDGE: Prepare Dark Chocolate Fudge as directed, substituting 2 packages (10 ounces each) peanut butter chips for the semisweet chocolate chips.

Makes about 2¼ pounds or 64 candies

Top Box: *Dark Chocolate Fudge and Peanut Butter Fudge;*
Middle Box: *Traditional Peanut Brittle*

POPCORN CRUNCHIES

- 12 cups popped popcorn (about ¾ cup unpopped)
- 1½ cups sugar
- ⅓ cup water
- ⅓ cup corn syrup
- 2 tablespoons butter or margarine
- 1 teaspoon vanilla

Preheat oven to 250°F. Grease large shallow roasting pan. Add popcorn. Keep warm in oven while making caramel mixture.

Place sugar, water and corn syrup in heavy 2-quart saucepan. Stir over low heat until sugar has dissolved and mixture comes to a boil. Carefully clip candy thermometer to side of pan (do not let bulb touch bottom of pan). Cook over low heat about 10 minutes or until thermometer registers 280°F, without stirring. Occasionally wash down any sugar crystals that form on side of the pan using pastry brush dipped in warm water. Immediately remove from heat. Stir in butter and vanilla until smooth.

Pour hot syrup mixture slowly over warm popcorn, turning to coat kernels evenly. Set aside until cool enough to handle but warm enough to shape. Butter hands. Working quickly, lightly press warm mixture into 2-inch balls. Cool completely. Store in airtight container.

Makes about 14 popcorn balls

TIPS: If making Popcorn Crunchies to eat, insert lollipop sticks while still warm; set aside to cool completely. Cover with decorative plastic wrap. If making Popcorn Crunchies for tree ornaments, cool balls completely and wrap each ball with enough decorative plastic wrap to pull wrap together at top. Secure with a ribbon which can be formed into a bow or a loop for hanging.

HERSHEY®'S VANILLA MILK CHIPS ALMOND FUDGE

- 1⅔ cups (10-ounce package) HERSHEY®'S Vanilla Milk Chips
- ⅔ cup sweetened condensed milk (not evaporated milk)
- 1½ cups coarsely chopped slivered almonds, toasted*
- ½ teaspoon vanilla extract

*To toast almonds, spread almonds on cookie sheet. Bake at 350°F 8 to 10 minutes or until lightly browned, stirring occasionally; cool.

Line 8-inch square pan with foil, extending foil over edges of pan. In medium saucepan over very low heat, melt vanilla milk chips with sweetened condensed milk, stirring constantly, until mixture is smooth. Remove from heat. Stir in almonds and vanilla. Spread into prepared pan. Cover; refrigerate 2 hours or until firm. Use foil to lift fudge out of pan; peel off foil. Cut fudge into squares.

Makes about 3 dozen pieces or 1½ pounds fudge

Popcorn Crunchies

TARYN

CHOCOLATE BUTTER CRUNCH

1 cup butter or margarine
1¼ cups sugar
¼ cup water
2 tablespoons light corn syrup
1 cup ground almonds, divided
½ teaspoon vanilla
¾ cup milk chocolate chips

Line 15½×10½×1-inch jelly-roll pan with foil, extending edges over sides of pan. Generously grease foil and narrow metal spatula with butter.

Melt butter in 2-quart saucepan over medium heat. Add sugar, water and corn syrup. Bring to a boil, stirring constantly.

Carefully clip candy thermometer to side of pan (do not let bulb touch bottom of pan). Cook until thermometer registers 290°F, stirring frequently. Stir in ⅔ cup almonds and vanilla. Pour into prepared pan. Spread mixture into corners with prepared spatula. Let stand 1 minute. Sprinkle with chocolate chips. Let stand 2 to 3 minutes more until chocolate melts. Spread chocolate over candy. Sprinkle with remaining ⅓ cup almonds. Cool completely.

Lift candy out of pan using foil; remove foil. Break candy into pieces. Store in airtight container.
Makes about 1½ pounds

MOCHA MARSHMALLOW FUDGE

1 tablespoon instant coffee
1 tablespoon boiling water
2½ cups sugar
½ cup butter or margarine
1 can (5 ounces) evaporated milk (⅔ cup)
1½ cups semisweet chocolate chips
1 jar (7 ounces) marshmallow creme
½ teaspoon vanilla

Line 9-inch square baking pan with foil, extending edges over sides of pan. Lightly grease foil with butter. Dissolve coffee in water; set aside.

Place sugar, butter and evaporated milk in 2-quart saucepan; bring to a boil over medium-high heat, stirring constantly. Reduce heat to medium. Continue boiling 5 minutes, stirring constantly. Remove from heat. Immediately stir in reserved coffee mixture, chocolate, marshmallow creme and vanilla. Pour into prepared pan. Let stand 1 hour.

Lift candy out of pan using foil; remove foil. Cut into 1-inch squares. Cover; refrigerate until fudge is set. *Makes about 2½ pounds or 64 pieces*

Top to bottom: *Mocha Marshmallow Fudge and Chocolate Butter Crunch*

MRS. CLAUS'S GREAT GRAPE GUMDROPS

- **1¼ cups sugar, divided**
- **1 cup light corn syrup**
- **¾ cup grape juice**
- **1 box (1¾ ounces) powdered fruit pectin**
- **½ teaspoon baking soda**
- **3 drops blue food coloring**

Line 9×5-inch loaf pan with foil, extending edges over sides of pan. Lightly grease foil with butter.

Bring 1 cup sugar and corn syrup to a boil in 2-quart saucepan over medium-low heat, stirring constantly. Carefully clip candy thermometer to side of pan (do not let bulb touch bottom of pan). Cook until thermometer registers 280°F, without stirring. Reduce heat to low.

Meanwhile, combine juice, pectin and baking soda in 3-quart saucepan. Bring to a boil over medium heat, stirring constantly. Boil 1 minute. Reduce heat to low; cook until thermometer registers 280°F.

Slowly pour hot pectin mixture into sugar mixture, stirring occasionally. (This should take about 2 minutes.) Remove from heat; stir in food coloring. Pour into prepared pan. Let stand at room temperature 24 hours.

Lift candy out of pan using foil; remove foil. Cut into squares using knife dipped into sugar. Roll squares in remaining ¼ cup sugar to coat and place on sheet of waxed paper. Let stand at room temperature 1 hour. Store in airtight container.

Makes about 1 pound or 64 gumdrops

MINT GUMDROPS: Prepare recipe as directed, substituting ¾ cup water for grape juice and 3 drops green food coloring for blue food coloring. Stir in ½ teaspoon peppermint extract with food coloring.

CHOCOLATE CHIP PEANUT BUTTER FUDGE

- **4 cups sugar**
- **1 jar (7 ounces) marshmallow creme**
- **1½ cups (12-ounce can) evaporated milk**
- **1 cup REESE'S® Creamy or Crunchy Peanut Butter**
- **1 tablespoon butter or margarine**
- **1 cup HERSHEY'®S Semi-Sweet Chocolate Chips or HERSHEY'®S Milk Chocolate Chips**

Line 13×9×2-inch pan with foil, extending foil over edges of pan. Butter foil lightly; set aside. In heavy 4-quart saucepan, stir together sugar, marshmallow creme, evaporated milk, peanut butter and butter. Cook over medium heat, stirring constantly, until mixture comes to a full rolling boil; boil 5 minutes, stirring constantly. Remove from heat. Immediately add chocolate chips; stir

until smooth. Pour into prepared pan; cool until firm. Use foil to lift fudge out of pan; peel off foil. Cut fudge into squares. Store in tightly covered container in cool, dry place.

Makes about 8 dozen pieces or 3½ pounds fudge

NOTE: For best results, do not double this recipe.

COAL CANDY

2 cups sugar
¾ cup light corn syrup
½ cup water
1 teaspoon anise extract
½ teaspoon black paste food coloring

Line 8-inch square baking pan with foil, extending edges over sides of pan. Lightly grease foil with butter.

Measure sugar, corn syrup and water into heavy 2-quart saucepan. Stir over medium-low heat until sugar is dissolved and mixture comes to a boil, being careful not to splash sugar mixture on side of pan. Carefully clip candy thermometer to side of pan (do not let bulb touch bottom of pan). Cook about 15 minutes until thermometer registers 290°F, without stirring. Immediately remove from heat. Stir in anise extract and food coloring. Pour mixture into prepared pan. Cool completely.

Lift candy out of pan using foil; remove foil. Place candy between 2 layers of heavy-duty foil. Pound with mallet to break candy into 1- to 2-inch pieces.

Makes about 1½ pounds

JOLLY BOURBON BALLS

1 package (12 ounces) vanilla wafers, finely crushed (3 cups)
1 cup finely chopped nuts
1 cup powdered sugar, divided
1 cup (6 ounces) semisweet chocolate chips
½ cup light corn syrup
⅓ cup bourbon or rum

Combine crushed wafers, nuts and ½ cup powdered sugar in large bowl; set aside.

Melt chocolate with corn syrup in top of double boiler over simmering (not boiling) water. Stir in bourbon until smooth. Pour chocolate mixture over crumb mixture; stir to combine thoroughly. Shape scant 1 tablespoonful of mixture into 1-inch ball. Repeat with remaining mixture. Roll balls in your palms to form uniform round shapes; place on waxed paper.

Place remaining ½ cup powdered sugar in shallow bowl. Roll balls in powdered sugar; place in petit four or candy cases. Store in airtight containers at least 3 days before serving for flavors to mellow. (May be stored up to 2 weeks.)

Makes about 48 candies

COUNTRY PECAN PIE

Pie pastry for single 9-inch pie crust
1¼ cups dark corn syrup
4 eggs
½ cup packed light brown sugar
¼ cup butter or margarine, melted
2 teaspoons all-purpose flour
1½ teaspoons vanilla
1½ cups pecan halves

Preheat oven to 350°F. Roll pastry on lightly floured surface to form 13-inch circle. Fit into 9-inch pie plate. Trim edges; flute. Set aside.

Combine corn syrup, eggs, brown sugar and butter in large bowl; beat with electric mixer at medium speed until well blended. Stir in flour and vanilla until blended. Pour into unbaked pie crust. Arrange pecans on top.

Bake 40 to 45 minutes until center of filling is puffed and golden brown. Cool completely on wire rack. Garnish as desired. *Makes one 9-inch pie*

CREAMY CHOCOLATE MARBLE CHEESECAKE

Cinnamon Graham Crust (recipe follows)
3 packages (8 ounces each) cream cheese, softened
¾ cup sugar
3 eggs
1 cup dairy sour cream
1 teaspoon vanilla
1 square (1 ounce) unsweetened chocolate, melted*

*For plain cheesecake, omit melted chocolate. Proceed as directed.

Preheat oven to 450°F. Prepare Cinnamon Graham Crust.

Beat cream cheese in large bowl with electric mixer at medium speed until fluffy. Beat in sugar until light and fluffy. Beat in eggs, 1 at a time, at low speed until well blended. Stir in sour cream and vanilla. Blend melted chocolate into 1 cup batter. Spoon plain and chocolate batters alternately over crust. Cut through batters several times with a knife for marble effect.

Bake 10 minutes. *Reduce oven temperature to 250°F.* Bake 30 minutes more or until center is just set. Remove pan to wire rack. Carefully loosen edge of cake with narrow knife. Cool completely on wire rack. Refrigerate several hours or overnight. To serve, place on plate. Carefully remove side of pan.

Makes one 9-inch cheesecake

Cinnamon Graham Crust

1 cup graham cracker crumbs
3 tablespoons sugar
½ teaspoon ground cinnamon
3 tablespoons butter or margarine, melted

Preheat oven to 350°F. Combine crumbs, sugar and cinnamon in small bowl. Stir in melted butter until blended. Press onto bottom of 9-inch springform pan. Bake 10 minutes. Cool on wire rack while preparing filling.

HOLIDAY EGGNOG PIE

1 package (4¾ ounces) vanilla pudding and pie filling mix
2 cups dairy eggnog
1¼ cups milk
1 tablespoon light rum
⅛ teaspoon ground nutmeg
Pastry for one 9-inch pie crust, baked
Whipped cream
Nutmeg

Cook mix according to package directions for pie filling, except using 2 cups eggnog and 1¼ cups milk. Stir in rum and nutmeg; pour into crust. Cover surface with plastic wrap; chill several hours. Garnish with whipped cream and nutmeg.

Makes 8 servings

Favorite recipe from **Wisconsin Milk Marketing Board**

Top to bottom: *Cheesecake (variation) and Creamy Chocolate Marble Cheesecake*

SOUR CREAM COFFEE CAKE WITH CHOCOLATE AND WALNUTS

- **¾ cup butter or margarine, softened**
- **1½ cups packed light brown sugar**
- **3 eggs**
- **2 teaspoons vanilla**
- **3 cups all-purpose flour**
- **2 teaspoons baking powder**
- **2 teaspoons ground cinnamon**
- **1½ teaspoons baking soda**
- **½ teaspoon ground nutmeg**
- **¼ teaspoon salt**
- **1½ cups dairy sour cream**
- **½ cup semisweet chocolate chips**
- **½ cup chopped walnuts**
- **Powdered sugar**

Preheat oven to 350°F. Grease and flour 12-cup Bundt pan or 10-inch tube pan. Beat butter in large bowl with electric mixer at medium speed until creamy. Add brown sugar; beat until light and fluffy. Beat in eggs and vanilla until well blended. Combine flour, baking powder, cinnamon, baking soda, nutmeg and salt in large bowl; add to butter mixture at low speed alternately with sour cream, beginning and ending with flour mixture until well blended. Stir in chocolate and walnuts. Spoon into prepared pan.

Bake 45 to 50 minutes until wooden pick inserted in center comes out clean. Cool in pan 15 minutes. Remove from pan to wire rack; cool completely. Store tightly covered at room temperature. Sprinkle with powdered sugar before serving.

Makes one 10-inch coffee cake

TINY SPICED CAKES

- **1 package (17 ounces) pound cake mix**
- **1 tablespoon apple pie spice**
- **¾ cup milk**
- **2 eggs**
- **1 cup diced unpeeled apple**
- **1 cup coarsely chopped walnuts**
- **2 cups powdered sugar**
- **5 to 6 teaspoons fresh lemon juice**

Preheat oven to 350°F. In large bowl of electric mixer, mix together cake mix and apple pie spice. Add milk and eggs; beat according to package directions until well mixed. Stir in apple and walnuts. Spoon into paper-lined 2½-inch cupcake pans, filling cups ⅔ full. Bake 20 to 25 minutes or until wooden pick inserted in center comes out clean. Cool on wire racks.

Meanwhile, in small bowl, mix powdered sugar with lemon juice. Spread frosting on top of cakes. Top with walnut halves and colored sugar, if desired. Store in tightly covered container up to 2 weeks or wrap securely and freeze.

Makes about 24 cupcakes

Favorite recipe from ***American Spice Trade Association***

Sour Cream Coffee Cake with Chocolate and Walnuts

CHOCOLATE CREAM-FILLED CAKE ROLL

- ¾ cup sifted cake flour
- ¼ cup unsweetened cocoa
- ½ teaspoon baking powder
- ¼ teaspoon salt
- 4 eggs
- ¾ cup granulated sugar
- 1 tablespoon water
- 1 teaspoon vanilla
- Powdered sugar
- Cream Filling (recipe follows)
- Chocolate Stars (recipe follows)
- Sweetened whipped cream
- Fresh raspberries and mint leaves for garnish

Preheat oven to 375°F. Grease bottom of 15½×10½×1-inch jelly-roll pan. Line with waxed paper. Grease paper and sides of pan; dust with flour. Combine flour, cocoa, baking powder and salt in small bowl; set aside. Beat eggs in medium bowl with electric mixer at high speed about 5 minutes or until thick and lemon colored. Add granulated sugar, a little at a time, beating well at medium speed; beat until thick and fluffy. Stir in water and vanilla. Fold in flour mixture until smooth. Spread into prepared pan.

Bake 12 to 15 minutes until wooden pick inserted in center comes out clean. Sprinkle towel with powdered sugar. Loosen cake edges and turn out onto prepared towel. Carefully peel off waxed paper. Roll up cake with towel inside, starting with narrow end. Cool, seam side down, 20 minutes on wire rack.

Meanwhile, prepare Cream Filling and Chocolate Stars. Unroll cake and spread with Cream Filling. Roll up again, without towel. Cover and refrigerate at least 1 hour before serving. Dust with additional powdered sugar before serving. Place star tip in pastry bag; add sweetened whipped cream. Pipe rosettes on top of cake. Place points of Chocolate Stars into rosettes. Garnish as desired. Store tightly covered in refrigerator.

Makes 8 to 10 servings

Cream Filling

- 1 teaspoon unflavored gelatin
- ¼ cup cold water
- 1 cup whipping cream
- 2 tablespoons powdered sugar
- 1 tablespoon orange-flavored liqueur

Sprinkle gelatin over cold water in small saucepan; let stand 1 minute. Heat over low heat until dissolved, stirring constantly. Cool to room temperature. Beat cream, powdered sugar and liqueur in small chilled bowl with electric mixer at high speed until stiff peaks form. Fold in gelatin mixture. Cover; refrigerate 5 to 10 minutes.

CHOCOLATE STARS: Melt 2 squares (1 ounce each) semisweet chocolate in heavy small saucepan over low heat, stirring frequently. Pour onto waxed paper-lined cookie sheet. Spread to ⅛-inch thickness with small metal spatula. Refrigerate about 15 minutes or until firm. Cut out stars with cookie cutter. Carefully lift stars from waxed paper using metal spatula or knife. Refrigerate until ready to use.

Chocolate Cream-Filled Cake Roll

KISS O'LEMON POUND CAKE

- 1 cup QUAKER® Oats (quick or old fashioned, uncooked)
- 1¾ cups all-purpose flour
- 1 teaspoon baking powder
- ½ teaspoon salt (optional)
- 1¼ cups sugar
- 1 cup (2 sticks) margarine or butter, softened
- 3 eggs
- 2 tablespoons grated lemon peel (about 3 lemons)
- ¾ cup milk
- Powdered sugar
- Additional grated lemon peel for garnish
- 1 package (10 ounces) frozen red raspberries, thawed

Heat oven to 350°F. Grease and lightly flour 9×5-inch loaf pan. Place oats in blender container; blend about 1 minute, stopping occasionally to stir. Combine with flour, baking powder and salt. Set aside. Beat sugar and margarine until fluffy. Add eggs and lemon peel; mix well. Add combined dry ingredients alternately with milk, mixing until well blended. Pour into prepared pan. Bake 1 hour 10 minutes or until toothpick inserted in center comes out clean. Cool 10 minutes in pan. Remove to wire rack; cool completely. Sprinkle with powdered sugar. Garnish with lemon peel, if desired. In blender, blend raspberries until smooth. Serve with pound cake.

Makes 16 servings

SPICY PUMPKIN PIE

- Pie pastry for single 9-inch pie crust
- 1 can (16 ounces) pumpkin (not pumpkin pie filling)
- ¾ cup packed light brown sugar
- 2 teaspoons ground cinnamon
- ¾ teaspoon ground ginger
- ½ teaspoon ground nutmeg
- ¼ teaspoon salt
- ⅛ teaspoon ground cloves
- 4 eggs, slightly beaten
- 1½ cups light cream or half-and-half
- 1 teaspoon vanilla
- Sweetened whipped cream

Preheat oven to 400°F. Roll pie pastry on lightly floured surface to form 13-inch circle. Fit into 9-inch pie plate. Trim edges; flute. Set aside.

Combine pumpkin and brown sugar in large bowl; mix well. Stir in cinnamon, ginger, nutmeg, salt and cloves. Add eggs; mix well. Gradually stir in cream and vanilla, mixing until combined. Pour pumpkin mixture into unbaked pie crust.

Bake 40 to 45 minutes until knife inserted near center comes out clean. Cool on wire rack. Serve warm topped with sweetened whipped cream.

Makes one 9-inch pie

Kiss O'Lemon Pound Cake

PEANUT BUTTER CHIP POUND CAKE WITH STREUSEL SWIRL

Streusel Swirl (recipe follows)
¾ cup (1½ sticks) butter or margarine, softened
1½ cups sugar
3 eggs
1 teaspoon vanilla extract
3 cups all-purpose flour
1½ teaspoons baking powder
1½ teaspoons baking soda
¼ teaspoon salt
1½ cups (12 ounces) dairy sour cream
1⅔ cups (10-ounce package) REESE'S® Peanut Butter Chips
Peanut Butter Creme Glaze (recipe follows)

Prepare Streusel Swirl. Heat oven to 350°F. Grease 12-cup fluted tube pan. In large mixer bowl, beat butter, sugar, eggs and vanilla until creamy. Stir together flour, baking powder, baking soda and salt; add alternately with sour cream to butter mixture, beating well after each addition. Stir in peanut butter chips. Spread half the batter into prepared pan. Sprinkle Streusel Swirl over batter. Carefully spread remaining batter over top. Bake 1 hour 5 minutes to 1 hour 10 minutes or until golden brown and wooden pick inserted in center comes out clean. Cool 15 minutes; remove from pan to wire rack. Cool completely. Prepare Peanut Butter Creme Glaze; drizzle over cake. Garnish as desired.

Makes 10 to 12 servings

Streusel Swirl

¼ cup packed brown sugar
¼ cup chopped nuts
½ teaspoon ground cinnamon

In small bowl, stir together brown sugar, nuts and cinnamon.

Peanut Butter Creme Glaze

⅓ cup sugar
¼ cup water
1 cup REESE'S® Peanut Butter Chips
2 tablespoons marshmallow creme

In small saucepan, heat sugar and water until mixture comes to a boil. Remove from heat. Immediately add peanut butter chips; stir until melted. Add marshmallow creme; beat until smooth and of desired consistency. Add additional hot water, ½ teaspoon at a time, if needed.

Top to bottom: *Peanut Butter Chip Pound Cake with Streusel Swirl, Chocolate Glazed Citrus Poppy Seed Cake (page 112) and Mini Chip Harvest Ring (page 112)*

MINI CHIP HARVEST RING

¾ cup whole-wheat flour*
¾ cup all-purpose flour
¾ cup granulated sugar
½ cup packed light brown sugar
2 teaspoons ground cinnamon
1¼ teaspoons baking soda
½ teaspoon salt
3 eggs
¾ cup vegetable oil
1½ teaspoons vanilla extract
2 cups grated carrots, apples or zucchini, drained
¾ cup HERSHEY®'S MINI CHIPS® Semi-Sweet Chocolate
½ cup chopped walnuts
Cream Cheese Glaze (recipe follows)

*All-purpose flour may be substituted for whole-wheat flour.

Heat oven to 350°F. Grease and flour 6- or 8-cup fluted tube pan. In large bowl, stir together whole-wheat flour, all-purpose flour, granulated sugar, brown sugar, cinnamon, baking soda and salt. In small bowl, beat eggs, oil and vanilla. Add to dry ingredients; blend well. Stir in carrots, small chocolate chips and walnuts. Pour batter into prepared pan. Bake 45 to 50 minutes or until wooden pick inserted in center comes out clean. Cool 30 minutes; remove from pan to wire rack. Prepare Cream Cheese Glaze; drizzle over top of cake, allowing glaze to run down sides. Garnish as desired. *Makes 8 to 10 servings*

Cream Cheese Glaze

1½ ounces (½ of 3-ounce package) cream cheese, softened
¾ cup powdered sugar
2 teaspoons milk
½ teaspoon vanilla extract

In small bowl, beat cream cheese, powdered sugar, milk and vanilla until smooth and of desired consistency. Add additional milk, ½ teaspoon at a time, if needed.

CHOCOLATE GLAZED CITRUS POPPY SEED CAKE

1 package (about 18 ounces) lemon cake mix
⅓ cup poppy seed
⅓ cup milk
3 eggs
1 container (8 ounces) plain lowfat yogurt
1 teaspoon freshly grated lemon peel
Chocolate Citrus Glaze (page 113)

Heat oven to 350°F. Grease and flour 12-cup fluted tube pan or 10-inch tube pan. In large mixer bowl, combine cake mix, poppy seed, milk, eggs, yogurt and lemon peel; beat until well blended. Pour batter into prepared pan. Bake 40 to 45 minutes or until wooden pick inserted in center comes out clean. Cool 20 minutes; remove from pan to wire rack. Cool completely. Prepare Chocolate Citrus Glaze; spoon over cake, allowing glaze to run down sides. *Makes 12 servings*

Chocolate Citrus Glaze

2 tablespoons butter or margarine
2 tablespoons HERSHEY®'S Cocoa or HERSHEY®'S European Style Cocoa
2 tablespoons water
1 tablespoon orange-flavored liqueur (optional)
½ teaspoon orange extract
1¼ to 1½ cups powdered sugar

In small saucepan over medium heat, melt butter. With whisk, stir in cocoa and water until mixture thickens slightly. Remove from heat; stir in liqueur, if desired, orange extract and 1¼ cups powdered sugar. Whisk until smooth. If glaze is too thin, whisk in remaining ¼ cup powdered sugar. Use immediately.

RUM AND SPUMONI LAYERED TORTE

1 package (18 to 19 ounces) moist butter yellow cake mix
3 eggs
½ cup butter or margarine, softened
⅓ cup plus 2 teaspoons rum, divided
⅓ cup water
1 quart spumoni ice cream, softened
1 cup whipping cream
1 tablespoon powdered sugar
Chopped mixed candied fruit
Red and green sugar for decorating (optional)

Preheat oven to 375°F. Grease and flour 15½×10½×1-inch jelly-roll pan. Combine cake mix, eggs, butter, ⅓ cup rum and water in large bowl. Beat with electric mixer at low speed until moistened. Beat at high speed 4 minutes. Pour evenly into prepared pan.

Bake 20 to 25 minutes until wooden pick inserted in center comes out clean. Cool in pan 10 minutes. Turn out of pan onto wire rack; cool completely.

Cut cake into three 10×5-inch pieces. Place one cake layer on serving plate. Spread with half the softened ice cream. Cover with second cake layer. Spread with remaining ice cream. Place remaining cake layer on top. Gently push down. Wrap cake in plastic wrap and freeze at least 4 hours.

Just before serving, combine cream, powdered sugar and remaining 2 teaspoons rum in small chilled bowl. Beat at high speed with chilled beaters until stiff peaks form. Remove cake from freezer. Spread thin layer of whipped cream mixture over *top* of cake. Place star tip in pastry bag; add remaining whipped cream mixture. Pipe rosettes around outer top edges of cake. Place candied fruit in narrow strip down center of cake. Sprinkle colored sugar over rosettes, if desired. Serve immediately. *Makes 8 to 10 servings*

GOLDEN HOLIDAY FRUITCAKE

- 1½ cups butter or margarine, softened
- 1½ cups sugar
- 6 eggs
- 2 teaspoons grated lemon peel
- 2 tablespoons fresh lemon juice
- 3 cups all-purpose flour
- 2 teaspoons baking powder
- ½ teaspoon baking soda
- ¼ teaspoon salt
- 1½ cups golden raisins
- 1½ cups pecan halves
- 1½ cups red and green candied pineapple chunks
- 1 cup dried apricot halves, cut in half
- 1 cup halved red candied cherries
- 1 cup halved green candied cherries
- Light corn syrup
- Candied and dried fruit and pecans, for garnish

Preheat oven to 325°F. Grease and flour 10-inch tube pan. Beat butter in large bowl with electric mixer at medium speed until creamy. Add sugar; beat until light and fluffy. Add eggs, 1 at a time, beating well after each addition. Stir in lemon peel and juice. Combine flour, baking powder, baking soda and salt in large bowl. Reserve ½ cup flour mixture. Gradually blend remaining flour mixture into butter mixture at low speed. Combine raisins, pecans, pineapple, apricots and cherries in large bowl. Toss fruit mixture with reserved ½ cup flour mixture. Stir fruit mixture into butter mixture. Spoon evenly into prepared pan.

Bake 80 to 90 minutes until wooden pick inserted in center comes out clean. Cool in pan 15 minutes. Remove from pan to wire rack; cool completely. Store up to 1 month tightly covered at room temperature. (If desired, cake may be stored wrapped in a wine- or brandy-soaked cloth in airtight container. Cake may be frozen up to 2 months.)

Before serving, lightly brush surface of cake with corn syrup. Arrange candied and dried fruit decoratively on top. Brush fruit with corn syrup.

Makes one 10-inch round fruitcake

Golden Holiday Fruitcake

ORANGE PUMPKIN TART

- 1½ cups all-purpose flour
- 1 cup QUAKER® Oats (quick or old fashioned, uncooked), divided
- 1 cup plus 2 tablespoons granulated sugar, divided
- ¾ cup (1½ sticks) margarine
- 2 tablespoons water
- 1 (16-ounce) can (1¾ cups) pumpkin
- 1 egg white
- 1 teaspoon pumpkin pie spice
- ½ cup powdered sugar
- 2 teaspoons orange juice
- ½ teaspoon grated orange peel

Preheat oven to 400°F. Combine flour, ¾ cup oats and ½ cup granulated sugar; cut in margarine until crumbly. Reserve ¾ cup mixture. Mix remaining oat mixture with water until moistened. Divide into 2 parts; press each onto cookie sheet to form 12×5-inch tart. Combine pumpkin, egg white, ½ cup granulated sugar and spice. Spread over tarts. Top with combined ¼ cup oats, 2 tablespoons granulated sugar and reserved oat mixture. Bake 25 minutes or until golden. Cool. Drizzle with combined remaining ingredients. Refrigerate leftovers. *Makes 12 servings*

FESTIVE MINCEMEAT TARTLETS

- Pastry for double pie crust
- 1½ cups prepared mincemeat
- ½ cup chopped peeled, cored tart apple
- ⅓ cup golden raisins
- ⅓ cup chopped walnuts
- 3 tablespoons brandy *or* apple juice concentrate
- 1 tablespoon grated lemon peel

Preheat oven to 400°F. Divide pastry in half. Refrigerate one half. Roll remaining half on lightly floured surface to form 13-inch circle. Cut six 4-inch rounds. Fit each pastry round into 2¾-inch muffin cup. Prick inside of crust with fork; set aside. Repeat with remaining pastry.

Bake unfilled pastry crusts 8 minutes. Meanwhile, combine mincemeat, apple, raisins, walnuts, brandy and lemon peel in medium bowl until well blended. Remove crusts from oven; fill each with rounded tablespoonful of mincemeat mixture. Press lightly into crust with back of spoon.

Bake 18 to 20 minutes more until crust edges are golden. Cool in pan 5 minutes. Carefully remove from pan to wire rack. Serve warm or cool completely. *Makes twelve 2¾-inch tartlets*

Orange Pumpkin Tarts

CRANBERRY APPLE NUT PIE

Rich Pie Pastry (recipe follows)
1 cup sugar
3 tablespoons all-purpose flour
¼ teaspoon salt
4 cups sliced peeled tart apples
2 cups fresh cranberries
½ cup golden raisins
½ cup coarsely chopped pecans
1 tablespoon grated lemon peel
2 tablespoons butter or margarine
1 egg, beaten

Preheat oven to 425°F. Divide dough in half. Roll half of pie pastry on lightly floured surface to form 13-inch circle. Fit into 9-inch pie plate; trim edges. Reroll scraps and cut into decorative shapes, such as holly leaves and berries, for garnish; set aside.

Combine sugar, flour and salt in large bowl. Stir in apples, cranberries, raisins, pecans and lemon peel; toss well. Spoon fruit mixture into unbaked pie crust. Dot with butter. Roll remaining half of pie pastry on lightly floured surface to form 11-inch circle. Place over filling. Trim and seal edges. Cut 3 slits in center of top crust. Moisten pastry cutouts and decorate as desired. Lightly brush top crust with egg.

Bake 35 to 40 minutes until apples are tender when pierced with a fork and pastry is golden brown. Cool in pan on wire rack. Serve warm or cool completely. *Makes one 9-inch pie*

Rich Pie Pastry

2 cups all-purpose flour
¼ teaspoon salt
6 tablespoons butter
6 tablespoons lard
6 to 8 tablespoons cold water

Combine flour and salt in medium bowl. Cut in butter and lard with pastry blender or 2 knives until mixture resembles coarse crumbs. Sprinkle water, 1 tablespoon at a time, over flour mixture, mixing until flour is moistened. Shape dough into a ball. Roll, fill and bake as recipe directs.
Makes pastry for one 9-inch double pie crust

NOTE: For single crust, cut recipe in half.

Cranberry Apple Nut Pie

DEEP DARK CHOCOLATE CAKE

2 cups sugar
1¾ cups all-purpose flour
¾ cup HERSHEY®'S Cocoa or HERSHEY®'S European Style Cocoa
1½ teaspoons baking powder
1½ teaspoons baking soda
1 teaspoon salt
2 eggs
1 cup milk
½ cup vegetable oil
2 teaspoons vanilla extract
1 cup boiling water
One-Bowl Buttercream Frosting (recipe follows)

Heat oven to 350°F. Grease and flour two 9-inch round cake pans.* In large mixer bowl, stir together sugar, flour, cocoa, baking powder, baking soda and salt. Add eggs, milk, oil and vanilla; beat on medium speed of electric mixer 2 minutes. Stir in water. (Batter will be thin.) Pour batter evenly into prepared pans. Bake 30 to 35 minutes or until wooden pick inserted in center comes out clean. Cool 10 minutes; remove from pans to wire racks. Cool completely. Prepare One-Bowl Buttercream Frosting; spread between layers and over top and side of cake. *Makes 8 to 10 servings*

*One 13×9×2-inch baking pan may be substituted for 9-inch cake pans. Prepare as directed. Bake 35 to 40 minutes. Cool completely in pan on wire rack. Frost as desired.

One-Bowl Buttercream Frosting

6 tablespoons butter or margarine, softened
2⅔ cups powdered sugar
½ cup HERSHEY®'S Cocoa
⅓ cup milk
1 teaspoon vanilla extract

In small mixer bowl, beat butter. Blend in powdered sugar and cocoa alternately with milk, beating well after each addition until smooth and of spreading consistency. Blend in vanilla. Add additional milk, if needed.

Deep Dark Chocolate Cake

PUMPKIN CHEESE–SWIRLED PIE

1 package (3 ounces) cream cheese, softened
½ cup KARO® Light Corn Syrup, divided
½ teaspoon vanilla
1 cup canned solid pack pumpkin
2 eggs
½ cup evaporated milk
¼ cup sugar
2 teaspoons pumpkin pie spice
¼ teaspoon salt
1 (9-inch) frozen deep-dish pie crust

Preheat oven to 325°F. In small bowl with mixer at medium speed, beat cream cheese until light and fluffy. Gradually beat in ¼ cup corn syrup and vanilla until smooth; set aside. In medium bowl, combine pumpkin, eggs, evaporated milk, remaining ¼ cup corn syrup, sugar, pumpkin pie spice and salt. Beat until smooth. Pour into pie crust. Drop tablespoonfuls of cream cheese mixture onto pumpkin filling. With knife or small spatula, swirl mixture to give marbled effect.

Bake 50 to 60 minutes or until knife inserted halfway between edge and center comes out clean. Cool completely on wire rack.

Makes 8 servings

Prep Time: 20 minutes
Bake Time: 50 minutes, plus cooling

ORANGE LOVER'S CAKE

1¼ cups sugar
½ cup (1 stick) margarine
2 eggs
½ cup orange juice
½ cup water
2 teaspoons grated orange peel
1¾ cups all-purpose flour
1 cup QUAKER® Oats (quick or old fashioned, uncooked)
2 teaspoons baking powder
½ teaspoon baking soda
½ teaspoon salt (optional)
½ cup powdered sugar
3 to 4 teaspoons orange juice
1 teaspoon grated orange peel

Heat oven to 350°F. Lightly spray 10-inch tube pan* with no-stick cooking spray or oil lightly. Beat sugar, margarine and eggs until fluffy. Blend in ½ cup orange juice, water and 2 teaspoons orange peel; mix well. Add combined flour, oats, baking powder, baking soda and salt; mix well. Pour into prepared pan. Bake 45 to 50 minutes or until golden brown. Cool 10 minutes in pan; remove to wire rack. Cool completely. Combine remaining ingredients; mixing until smooth. Drizzle over completely cooled cake. Store loosely covered.

Makes 12 servings

*Or substitute greased Bundt pan. Decrease baking time by 5 minutes; increase cooling time to 30 minutes before removing from pan.

Pumpkin Cheese-Swirled Pie

Acknowledgments

The publishers would like to thank the companies and organizations listed below for the use of their recipes and photographs in this publication.

American Spice Trade Association
Best Foods, a Division of CPC International Inc.
Bob Evans Farms®
Dole Food Company, Inc.
Heinz U.S.A.
Hershey Foods Corporation
Jones Dairy Farm
Lawry's® Foods, Inc.
McIlhenny Company
Minnesota Cultivated Wild Rice Council
Nestlé Food Company
Oscar Mayer Foods Corporation
The Quaker Oats Company
Refined Sugars Incorporated
The J.M. Smucker Company
The Sugar Association, Inc.
Wisconsin Milk Marketing Board

Index

METRIC CONVERSION CHART

VOLUME MEASUREMENTS (dry)

1/8 teaspoon = 0.5 mL
1/4 teaspoon = 1 mL
1/2 teaspoon = 2 mL
3/4 teaspoon = 4 mL
1 teaspoon = 5 mL
1 tablespoon = 15 mL
2 tablespoons = 30 mL
1/4 cup = 60 mL
1/3 cup = 75 mL
1/2 cup = 125 mL
2/3 cup = 150 mL
3/4 cup = 175 mL
1 cup = 250 mL
2 cups = 1 pint = 500 mL
3 cups = 750 mL
4 cups = 1 quart = 1 L

VOLUME MEASUREMENTS (fluid)

1 fluid ounce (2 tablespoons) = 30 mL
4 fluid ounces (1/2 cup) = 125 mL
8 fluid ounces (1 cup) = 250 mL
12 fluid ounces (1 1/2 cups) = 375 mL
16 fluid ounces (2 cups) = 500 mL

WEIGHTS (mass)

1/2 ounce = 15 g
1 ounce = 30 g
3 ounces = 90 g
4 ounces = 120 g
8 ounces = 225 g
10 ounces = 285 g
12 ounces = 360 g
16 ounces = 1 pound = 450 g

DIMENSIONS

1/16 inch = 2 mm
1/8 inch = 3 mm
1/4 inch = 6 mm
1/2 inch = 1.5 cm
3/4 inch = 2 cm
1 inch = 2.5 cm

OVEN TEMPERATURES

250°F = 120°C
275°F = 140°C
300°F = 150°C
325°F = 160°C
350°F = 180°C
375°F = 190°C
400°F = 200°C
425°F = 220°C
450°F = 230°C

BAKING PAN SIZES

Utensil	Size in Inches/Quarts	Metric Volume	Size in Centimeters
Baking or Cake Pan (square or rectangular)	8×8×2	2 L	20×20×5
	9×9×2	2.5 L	22×22×5
	12×8×2	3 L	30×20×5
	13×9×2	3.5 L	33×23×5
Loaf Pan	8×4×3	1.5 L	20×10×7
	9×5×3	2 L	23×13×7
Round Layer Cake Pan	8×1½	1.2 L	20×4
	9×1½	1.5 L	23×4
Pie Plate	8×1¼	750 mL	20×3
	9×1¼	1 L	23×3
Baking Dish or Casserole	1 quart	1 L	—
	1½ quart	1.5 L	—
	2 quart	2 L	—